Advance Praise for *Falling into the Arms of God*

"Megan Don has made this sixteenth-century mystic come alive for the twenty-first century. She makes Teresa of Avila fully accessible to our modern understanding, and she rightly perceives that our hunger today is to experience the divine, not only to 'believe' in it. This book shows us how we can begin that journey."

— David Tacey, PhD, author of
The Spirituality Revolution

"Megan Don's gentle and insightful reflections on the well-chosen excerpts from St. Teresa's works bring the reader and seeker more deeply into the quiet power and peace of real spiritual growth and intimacy with God."

— Amy Welborn, author of *The Words We Pray: Discovering the Richness of Traditional Catholic Prayer*

"In today's polluted cultural atmosphere, this book provides a breath of fresh air. Through her familiarity with the writings of the great Teresa and her keen psychological perceptions, Megan Don gently guides us to the center of our being and prayerfully invites us to breathe more deeply there. Clarity of expression nicely serves the luminous vision of this beautiful book."

— Anthony Kelly, professor,
Graduate School of Philosophy and Theology,
Australian Catholic University

"*Falling into the Arms of God* is guaranteed to deepen the spiritual experience and enrich the daily life of any spiritual seeker. It is especially helpful for those who, like Teresa of Avila, have active, full lives in the world and desire above all else to express the Will of God."

— Reverend Mary Omwake,
Unity minister on Maui

*f*ALLING
INTO THE
ARMS
OF GOD

fALLING INTO THE ARMS OF GOD

MEDITATIONS WITH TERESA OF AVILA

MEGAN DON

New World Library
Novato, California

New World Library
14 Pamaron Way
Novato, California 94949

Copyright © 2005 by Megan Don

For permissions acknowledgments, please see page 237.
All scripture quotations are from the New Jerusalem Bible.

Front cover design by Bill Mifsud
Text design and typography by Tona Pearce Myers

Library of Congress Cataloging-in-Publication Data
Don, Megan.
   Falling into the arms of God : meditations with Teresa of Avila
/ Megan Don.— 1st ed.
       p.   cm.
Includes bibliographical references.
ISBN 1-57731-484-0 (hardcover : alk. paper)
1. Teresa, of Avila, Saint, 1515–1582—Meditations. I. Title.
BX4700.T4D62 2005
242—dc22   2004026459

First printing, April 2005
ISBN 1-57731-484-0
ISBN-13 978-1-57731-484-4

Printed in Canada on partially recycled, acid-free paper

Distributed to the trade by Publishers Group West

10 9 8 7 6 5 4 3 2 1

To the God within us all

Contents

Third Dwelling: Self-Knowledge

Fourth Dwelling: Interior Recollection

Fifth Dwelling: Surrender

Sixth Dwelling: The Betrothal

Seventh Dwelling: The Sacred Marriage

Introduction

*Within oneself, very clearly, is the best place to look
[for God] . . . and it's not necessary to go to heaven,
nor any further than our own selves; for to do so is
to tire the spirit and distract the soul, without gaining
as much fruit.* (Collected Works *vol. I, 357)*

TERESA OF AVILA UNDERSTOOD that the mystery of
the divine indwelling was available to all people. For
her, contemplation was not restricted to nuns and
monks. Likewise, she believed that engaging in an
active life was not confined to those living in the sec-
ular world. Teresa's life provides us with an exceptional
example of bringing the contemplative and active life
together; it displays both a profound internal depth and
an exceptionally productive outcome.

Of both Jewish and Christian ancestry, Teresa de
Ahumada was born in Avila, Spain, in 1515, where she
had a privileged upbringing and belonged to the Spanish nobility. Societal status was extremely important in

sixteenth-century Spain, and Teresa's life was deeply affected by social expectations. She was also greatly influenced, however, by the religious ethos within her family, and consequently a certain dichotomous relationship was firmly established in Teresa's psyche. This dichotomy was to plague Teresa for many years to come.

At the age of twenty, after much deliberation, she chose to enter the Carmelite Monastery in Avila. She did not make this choice because of a vocational "calling" but because Teresa understood it to be a favorable alternative to marriage. Likewise, her choice of religious order was not owing to any spiritual affiliation but was simply made because a friend of hers had recently entered the order, and she thought it would be fun to be there together.

Her fascination with the world continued while she lived in the monastery, since it was not an enclosed order, and a stream of visitors occupied much of her time as they relayed the latest gossip, fashions, and news of the town. Prayers were ordered and recited by rote, which left her soul dry and uninspired. She attempted to enter her own "prayer of quiet," but finding the thoughts in her head far too noisy and disturbing, she gave up any attempt to develop a more meaningful way to pray. Her relationship with God at this time was fairly superficial.

For twenty years she lived a divided life. On the one hand her ego desired worldly attachments, while on the other her spirit was calling her to a deeper communion with God. At the age of forty, Teresa finally surrendered completely to God. Her real life and work had begun. She returned to her prayer of quiet, allowing God to lead her, no longer relying on her own techniques. Meditation became essential to Teresa in establishing a clear and firm foundation with God, and as she walked further on her spiritual pathway, she came to understand that this external God also "rests within." It was to this place that she would constantly return to receive guidance, love, and a feeling of deep peace that she could not find elsewhere.

In 1560 Teresa was guided to reform the Carmelite Order, both male and female. She chose John of the Cross (1542–1591) to become the first friar. John had studied with the Jesuits and had a promising academic career, but he unexpectedly entered the contemplative Carmelite Order. He was to become a great Spanish mystic and saint. Teresa introduced him to her teachings, of returning to the essence of the hermit fathers from Mt. Carmel in Israel, that is, of becoming "a garden of contemplation." She encountered numerous objections and hostilities, both from within and outside the order, and was thrown into fear and self-doubt. Teresa battled with this self-doubt for many years, but with continued faith in her inner God-self, she fought long and hard against the many male clerics who ceaselessly tried to invalidate her spiritual experiences. Through this she became an advocate for inner self-guidance.

Teresa created seventeen new monasteries altogether, traveling the length and breadth of Spain in often appalling conditions — encountering treacherous floods and heavy snowfalls, often housed in roadside inns with all kinds of villains and vermin. When asked what hell was like, Teresa quickly replied, "Hell is like a night in a bad hotel."

Through founding these monasteries, Teresa became an astute businesswoman. She raised funds to purchase properties, was conversant with tax laws, and even knew how to legally evade certain land taxes. Her diplomatic and bureaucratic skills were constantly called on as she dealt with nobility and local government officials. On one occasion she even had to ask the king of Spain for a personal favor. She was, as we would say today, a very modern woman.

Teresa has given us numerous volumes of writing in which she described her profoundly rich inner life. Her masterwork, *The Interior Castle,* one of the most celebrated books on mystical theology ever written, is a detailed guide for the journey toward spiritual perfection. In this work, she likened the soul to a crystal castle within which are seven dwelling places. Each dwelling place has many rooms and represents certain aspects of the spiritual journey: "In each of these there are many others, below and above and to the sides, with lovely gardens and fountains and labyrinths, such delightful things that you would want to be dissolved in praises of the great God who created the soul in His own image and likeness" (*Collected Works* vol. II, 452). She knew the beauty and wonder of her own soul and tirelessly instructed those in her monasteries and surrounding communities. She taught them how to enter deeply into this great mystery, ultimately leading to the center of the castle — the place where God resides.

In this book I provide a reflective interpretation, relevant to our twenty-first-century psychology and spirituality, of *The Interior Castle* and its seven dwellings. Teresa did not name the dwellings, and so I have given them titles suggested by her writing and according to my interpretation of the journey we embark on as we enter each dwelling place. As we travel with Teresa deeper into the center of our being, the spiritual journey becomes at once more demanding and more sublime. I also draw from her other autobiographical writings, such as *The Life,* and from her letters.

Throughout her work, Teresa wrote mainly about the nature of the soul. Only briefly did she delineate between the "soul" and "spirit." Writing late in life, she noted that as her daily duties continued, she felt a part of herself always remaining in the divine center, while the soul and all its faculties attended to necessary business. She believed it is the spirit that is one with God, even though paradoxically there is no separation between soul and spirit. She quotes St. Paul: "He that is joined or united to the Lord becomes one spirit with him." Her philosophical musings were short, however, since she was far more concerned with the practical application of her experiences, and she ends her brief foray into these thoughts by claiming the complex subtlety of our interior workings. In keeping with Teresa's use of it, the word *soul,* then, is to be read as defining the whole being.

Teresa often lamented over the ineptitude of language when trying to describe the divine and her experiences. Even though she was naturally influenced by the language of her day, her writings clearly indicate that her knowledge of the Supreme Reality went far beyond the linguistic limitations we are all faced with. In keeping with the tradition of Teresa's time and her writings, I have referred to God as He. Please read the name of God as whatever is comfortable for you, whether it be Spirit, Universe, Higher Power, or Energy. And please read the gender however it feels most comfortable to you, whether it be She, He, or It.

Teresa did not use the word *ego* but referred to her mind, will, and pride as creating havoc in her life through self-serving impulses such as personal demands and desires, fears and worries, and self-righteousness. Nonetheless, throughout this book I use the terms *ego* and the *smaller ego-self* when referring to such impulses, both Teresa's and our own, since they capture well her meaning and since modern readers can easily relate to these concepts.

Teresa passed from this world on October 15, 1582, at the age of sixty-eight. Her body was said to give off the perfume of roses, and it did not decompose. She was canonized as a saint on March 12, 1622.

Teresa had no time for a disembodied spirituality, and she would frequently say, "God preserve me from saintly people." She displayed much courage, heart, and humor and was able to balance an active and keen intellect with the surrender of the self to God. This is why I feel that she has much to teach us. Being principally a people driven by our thinking minds, we can appreciate and learn from her balanced life of surrender. We can enter into our own innate relationship with God, while simultaneously using and cultivating our intellects to further our work here on earth, whatever that is destined to be.

How to Read This Book

For the Individual Reader

Falling into the Arms of God consists of seven parts, or dwellings, each of which contains several brief chapters. This book may be read in two ways. The first is sequentially: by reading meditations consecutively, you will be taken on a journey that continually deepens your spiritual experience and your daily living. Try not to give yourself time limits when reading the book, since one meditation may especially inspire you, requiring you to stay with it for a week, a month, or more. Remember, Teresa spent her whole life journeying on this pathway.

The second way to read this book is through random selection. Sit quietly and allow yourself to come into a place of stillness; ask to be guided to the particular meditation that is relevant for you in that very moment. Teresa was a firm believer in this method of guidance and inspiration.

Whichever way you choose to read the book, try to find a quiet place where you will not be disturbed. Come to the reading with a sense of sacredness, both for yourself and for the divine. Give yourself time to breathe and to release your previous activities. Familiarize yourself with the theme that you are reading about — located at the beginning of each of the seven dwellings — then turn to the relevant meditation. Ask that your whole being be open to receiving what you need, and then proceed to read.

Each brief chapter consists of a quote from Teresa's writing, some reflective words, and then a meditation. I suggest that you first read the quote from Teresa's writing, then the reflective words, allowing your own experiences, thoughts, and feelings to arise as you read. Go back to the quote and read the words slowly and deliberately, letting them penetrate deeply within. Turn to the meditation at the end of each reflection and read it through. Then prepare yourself for actively *entering* the meditation. Make sure you are seated comfortably; begin by inhaling and exhaling very slowly, and feel yourself entering a state of deep relaxation. Gently return to the meditation and follow the guidance, at the same time allowing the spirit to take you to the divinely desired and relevant place for you.

Enjoy your journey!

For Group Study

This book is well suited to study and discussion groups. I suggest using the following format.

Make a commitment to yourself, to God, and to the group for fourteen weeks (three and a half months). Present and work with one reflection and meditation a week. Owing to the large number of reflections in this book, the group will need to limit its study to two chapters from each dwelling. For example, the first week, from part 1, you could choose "What Is Real?"; the second week you could choose "The Mystery," also from part 1. The third week, from part 2, you could choose "Inclined to Love"; the fourth week, also from part 2, you could choose "The Doubting Mind," and so on through all the dwellings.

Each week a different member of the group will choose the reflection to be studied and lead the group in the following suggested way. Begin the group with a short prayer welcoming all the members and inviting the spirit to be with you and to guide you on your journey of discovery and discussion. Allow time for all members to come into deep relaxation through breathing and silence. (You may wish to conduct a short breathing meditation by simply following the breath through inhalation and exhalation). When the group has reached a place of stillness in body and mind, read Teresa's quote from the chosen reflection. You may choose to read the quote twice. Then continue to read the reflection that follows it.

Once the reflection has been read, you may open the group for discussion, allowing members to speak about their thoughts and any issues that may arise from the reading. Let respect be your leader as all come forward with their concerns. When all contributions to the discussion have ended, lead the group back into the breath and into silence.

Slowly repeat the quote and lead the meditation as outlined, allowing time and space for the words to become an *active and living* meditation. The leader will then close the group when it feels appropriate, with a blessing for all in the group, for their families, and for the world, giving gratitude for the ageless wisdom available to us.

The above is a recommended format only and may be altered according to each group's need, desire, and inspiration. This author is available to conduct spiritual retreats and workshops based on this text. If your study group is interested please visit www.teresaofavilaretreats.com or email teresaretreats@yahoo.com.

I gathered the quotations from four sources, and from this point on, I indicate these sources parenthetically using the following abbreviations: *CW* for *The Collected Works of Teresa of Avila* (in three volumes); *TL* for *The Life of Saint Teresa of Avila by Herself; IC* for *The Interior Castle;* and *Letters* for *The Letters of St. Teresa.* In some cases the quotations are taken from my own translation of the Spanish of the *Collected Works,* and I reference these instances with the abbreviation AT, *CW.* The abbreviations are followed by volume numbers, where applicable, abbreviated as vol. I, vol. II, or vol. III, and page numbers. Throughout the book I also quote from the New Jerusalem Bible.

fALLING
INTO THE
ARMS
OF GOD

First Dwelling

THE AWAKENING

For often when a person is distracted and forgetful of God,
His Majesty will awaken it. (CW vol. II, 367)

We are constantly being given opportunities to reawaken, that is, to remember who we are — divine children of God. Teresa reminded us that this awakening occurs throughout our lifetimes and is not a once-or-twice-only opportunity; rather, it occurs every day in our lives. These awakenings come as moments, alone or with others, and they are divine offerings from God.

In this dwelling we are introduced to that "other reality" of our being, the ever-present mystical self. We are asked to look beyond the superficiality of our existence and to take notice of what lies deep within. Teresa wrote about the spiritual knowing of our childhood and about how so many of us become disengaged from it. She calls us back to our divine origins — to the great mystery and beauty of our souls.

1. The Mystical Reality

Oh children of the earth!
How long will you be hard of heart? (CW vol. I, 445)

THESE WORDS WERE SPOKEN TO TERESA by God when she was questioning the authenticity of her mystical experiences. In probing the nature of reality, we tend to gravitate toward the theory that the common experience should dictate our own: "After all, this is what the majority of people are living and experiencing, therefore it must be true." But what of the rare mystical experience? The validity of such an encounter needs to be recognized for what it is: a divine gift of love, which expands the human soul, enabling it to comprehend a greater reality.

We are all mystics slowly awakening to the reality of who we really are; that is, we are the children of heaven and earth, of spirit and matter, who are blessed both with heavenly and earthly experiences. God does not know the difference between these worlds, and we are all being given the opportunity to enter into this unity, if only we will soften our hearts and cease to question God's infinite ways. The way of the mystic is a pathway to experiencing these ways of infinity, a pathway open to all.

Teresa described one of her experiences as a fire being enkindled in her heart, coming, she said, from God's true love. She knew that this was not of her own doing, as she felt it consuming her and burning away old pains and miseries, with her soul emerging transformed like a phoenix rising from the ashes. Her soul possessed a fresh purity, and she began walking on the pathway again with new vision. Even so, she questioned its reality. Like Teresa, we too often doubt our experiences that bring us into a mystical closeness with our own souls and with God.

The soul contains a complex array of all our faculties, including memories, rational thought, and intuitive and psychic abilities. To have all these faculties come into alignment on an issue is often a very difficult task. For many, the rational mind is dominant, and subsequently it governs the process of interpretation and belief. For a few, the intuitive and psychic faculties are well developed, and so their belief system has been constructed accordingly. Most people do not experience a balance among all these faculties. The universal paradigm of the mystic, however, is one of unity, encompassing *all* faculties and realities, both inner and outer.

How do we experience this unification that the true mystic experiences? Through surrendering to the spirit, wrote Teresa. The spirit of God, which is *our* very spirit, lays all the faculties of the soul to rest in a unified existence of peace and love, and in doing so, allows the transformation of the soul to occur. Herein lies the true nature of the mystic — a unity of being known through a spiritual metamorphosis. Further, the word *mystic* derives from the Latin *mysterium,* which means "to be altered."

In time we will come to know our mystical experiences to be as valid as any other experience in our lives. We will no longer think of them as rare occurrences for a select few, but as a natural way of life for us all.

Meditation

Bring yourself into a quiet and reflective space. Follow the rhythm of your breath — breathe deeper and deeper into yourself. Allow thoughts and feelings to float by. Bring yourself before the spirit of God and lay your soul down. Immerse yourself in the calm, peace, and love. Allow your soul to be transformed — allow yourself to be.

2. God's Eyes

*These are favored children. He would not want them to
leave His side, nor does He leave them. . . . He seats them
at His table, He shares with them His food even to the
point of taking a portion from His own mouth to give them.*
(CW *vol. II, 97*)

SMALL CHILDREN ARE STILL VERY CLOSE TO GOD. Our
divine origins are reflected in their eyes, through their
feelings, and through their interaction with the world.
They carry the message of love so innocently and spontaneously, lightening the hearts of those around them.
They remind us of who we are.

When a baby or child looks at you, she is seeing
into your soul. Her gaze is not tempered by sentimentality or societal protocol but truly reflects the "love, as
strong as death" (Song of Songs 8:6). In our society love
has become equated with sentimental placations. But to
make another feel better is not always an act of love.
Love is not something to be done, but rather a pure

state of being, lived in truthfulness. A child looking into your eyes will engage you at this level if you allow him to, if you do not fall into condescending baby talk. Remember, children are wise beings who come straight from God, with their memory of the divine still intact. We would do well to give them room to communicate with us and to listen very carefully to what they are saying. We are blessed when we allow their truth to ignite our own.

Teresa believed in the child's innate ability to relate directly with God and thought that parents should encourage this at all times. She understood the initial childhood years as providing the foundation for that soul's life to emerge. She noted that it is not simply the parents' words but also the state of their soul and their very way of being that leave an indelible impression on the new soul entering this physical realm. Teresa was greatly influenced by her father in her early years, and his religious nature made such an impression on her that at the age of seven she ran away from home to become a martyr for God. Fortunately, an uncle caught her as she was leaving the city and foiled this plan!

As our society becomes more open to spiritual phenomena we can allow a child's story to help us on our journey. Children see through the eyes of God, and many see beyond the physical realm. A child's imaginary friends are now being recognized as beings from the other worlds — angels, deceased relatives, and so on. We too can regain our godly sight by innocently opening ourselves and seeing beyond who and what we think we are. We can return to an expansiveness of soul that is our divine and human heritage, to a soul that is innately loving and spontaneous and free.

Children are spiritual beings growing into their physicality, and adults are fully physical beings rediscovering their spirituality. Coming into a joint learning, we are given the opportunity once more to be fed by God, and to look once more with God's eyes, seeing the divine in ourselves and in everyone around us.

Meditation

Take time to sit in stillness. Call forth the innocence of your child self. Remember what it was like to feel the expansiveness of life, when each moment was an exploration and adventure. Let your eyes begin to see with this innocence, with this wonder. Look at yourself and at those around you. See your innate wisdom and that of others. Open yourself to the strength of love and to your ability to live it.

3. Blurry Vision

For now I realize what a danger it is at an age when one should begin to cultivate the virtues to associate with people who do not know the vanity of the world but rather are just getting ready to throw themselves into it. (CW vol. I, 57)

TERESA MOVED FROM HER SAINTLY childhood desires to an adolescent romanticism that was inspired by the chivalrous literature of the time. She spent her days voraciously reading romantic novels and, along with her cousins, dressed in the finest of clothes and jewelry. This behavior befitted her social status and was also demanded of any young woman intent on finding a suitor. Teresa was focused on societal and personal honor, with the ways of the world seeming far more exciting than the life of spiritual martyrdom that had previously inspired her. Owing to dubious relations with a particular cousin, however, her father arranged for Teresa to be sent to an Augustinian convent, where she stayed for a year, much to her chagrin.

In her autobiography, Teresa mentions repeatedly the importance of good companionship and talks about how easy it is to be misled by others, especially during adolescence. She remembers the innocence of her childhood and how quickly it eroded when she imitated her friends. When we too do this, our original godly vision becomes blurry and desires become distorted, with the soul beginning its journey into a state of confusion and lack of fulfillment.

The adolescence that Teresa wrote about does not just relate to teenagers but also to adults in their spiritual adolescence. This is the time when we become awakened to the reality of our true nature waiting to be reborn. We may catch glimpses of this marvelous being that we are, but like an adolescent moving back and forth between the childhood and the adult realms, we too alternate between the old society-formed self and the newly emerging inner God-self. It is necessary, advised Teresa, to be vigilant about how this birthing process unfolds. We need to take care when choosing the people we associate with. This is not a call to be judgmental of others but rather to make a choice that will enable us to grow to our greatest potential.

Good companionship can be both supportive and instructive. We must remember, however, that our friends do not always truly support our spiritual growth. In fact, very often they can reinforce our patterns of dependency or insecurity or our inability to be intimate. In turn we may also be supporting their particular psychological and/or spiritual patterns. What can begin as a feeling of union and delight at being understood can easily lapse into a relationship that is binding and unable to promote spiritual growth.

Virtue is not a word that rolls easily off the contemporary tongue. For many it is associated with morality or uprightness; however, it has also been defined as "inherent power" (*Collins English Dictionary*). For Teresa the greatest virtue was the growth of our soul; by attending to this growth, she believed, we can discover the power that we are all born with. Be vigilant, she warned. Watch closely as you grow into yourself spiritually, and allow for change and growth to occur both in your friends and in you. Too often we want people to stay the same to ensure our own comfort. Likewise, our growth may not always be welcomed even by those closest to us.

Meditation

Falling into a great and loving silence, allow your loved ones to greet you. Without the need for judgment or action simply let them speak to you — let the truth of their interaction become clear to you. Bless them all with love, and offer them to your divine self, asking that the greatest good for all come to be.

4. Dwelling Place

As to what good qualities there may be in our souls, or Who dwells within them, or how precious they are — those are things which we seldom consider and so we trouble little about carefully preserving the soul's beauty. (IC, 29)

TERESA OFTEN LAMENTED the fact that we do not understand ourselves or know who we are. Becoming so bound up with our worldly identity, we forget about our divine nature. She used the example of our family life to illustrate her point. What if, she asked, having spent so many years as part of a family, we were unable to know who we were? What if we didn't know our name, who our mother and father was, or which town or country we lived in? What can we tell of our divine origins? To say we have souls because our religious traditions have told us so is not good enough; we must actively enquire about, uncover, and come to know our souls.

Comparing the soul to a clear crystal castle with many rooms, Teresa wrote that there are "some above, others below, others at each side; and in the center and midst of them all is the chief mansion where the most secret things pass between God and the soul" (*IC,* 29). It is our divine responsibility, she maintained, to explore this castle, to come to know who resides at its center. And it is our responsibility to persevere with this ongoing discovery and eternal relationship that exists with our divine self. It is our duty to recognize how truly precious we are and to see all other beings as equally precious.

This is not a linear journey from the outer rooms to the center room. No, this journey is an eternal spiral. Sometimes we enter the room of past wounds, sometimes the room of peaceful meditation — there is no room where the door becomes closed, no matter how far we advance on our spiritual path. The room of humility is always ready for us to enter, and so too is the room where we see and know that we are a blessed child of God.

Teresa wrote, "There are many ways of *being*" (*IC,* 31). If we are intent on discovering our true nature, then we must also be prepared to enter all the rooms. To be sure, some will be more pleasant than others. But no matter what we discover about ourselves, we must remember that in the eyes of God, there is nothing wrong with us, and there never has been.

Too often our journey of self-discovery can become a complex psychological web, with our smaller ego-self (that place where self-serving impulses arise) becoming discouraged at its own ineptness or inability to love. The good news is that loving, whether it be of self or of another, is not its job; it is our larger God-self that fills our whole being with love. The ego need not do anything but simply allow the love to flow through. It is not by doing that love "gets done"; rather, it is by being that love simply happens.

Meditation

Falling into a place of peaceful being, let all thoughts subside. Imagine before you a beautiful crystal castle; see how it reflects all spectrums of light. Allow yourself to wander through this castle without any desire or agenda, simply being and flowing in the love emanating from the center. Let yourself be absorbed by this love, and look at your own preciousness in the same way that God looks at you.

5. The Shining Sun

It should be kept in mind here that the fount, the shining sun that is in the center of the soul, does not lose its beauty and splendor; it is always present in the soul, and nothing can take away its loveliness. But if a black cloth is placed over a crystal that is in the sun, obviously the sun's brilliance will have no effect on the crystal even though the sun is shining on it. (CW vol. II, 289)

TERESA WAS SHOWN THE BRILLIANCE of the castle, how a sun was shining in the center, its light spreading to all rooms. But she also saw that the outer rooms of the castle had little light and that the further away they were from the center, the darker they became. She was aware that although the light continued to shine, it was as if the soul was unable to enjoy and partake of its great brilliance and beauty. How sad, she said, for a soul to be separated from the light, how disturbed the senses became when deprived of their life-giving source.

In what ways do we separate ourselves from the shining sun? One of the most common ways to dull this inner sun is by failing to give love. And when we are not giving love it is usually because we are too absorbed in our own needs. It is not only others who may be hurt by our inattentiveness or lack of action. We are also hurt when we fail to connect with the light of God. This disconnection, wrote Teresa, can occur in many ways: we can become too engrossed in our work, we can become filled with self-importance, or we can simply become overly absorbed with our own needs and wants.

In failing to connect with God's light we come to notice how we then fail to relate with others. The black cloth becomes draped over our castle, blocking the light from penetrating through to our relationships. When the light is blocked, love is unable to flow. By concentrating too much on our work we barely have time for those we are closest to, let alone new relation-ships that may be waiting to evolve. In failing to acknowledge the divine in our life and seeing ourselves as the main protagonist, we may fall into arrogance, which can then estrange us from colleagues and friends. And by becoming absorbed with our own needs and wants we do not see the needs of others.

Sometimes drastic measures are needed before the black cloth can be removed, such as divorce or being fired from a job. However, by taking responsibility for the removal of our own cloth, we can invoke gentle responses and changes in our lives without the neces-sity for shocking disruptions. We can do this by devel-oping a connection or reconnection to the divine; it is a constant process that we can lovingly and willingly enter. Many may feel like too much effort is required, that the task is just too difficult. Yet Teresa believed that we spend too much time trying to achieve things ourselves, when God can bring things to fulfillment in a moment, if we only choose to ask.

Do we wish to allow the shining sun to penetrate through to all our rooms, or do we secretly nurture some of the darker ones? Let us pray for the illusion of darkness to be shed and for the eternal light to shine from deep within our souls, nurturing us and those we meet on our journey.

Meditation

Imagine looking at your inner castle. Feel the sun's brilliance as it shines from the center. Slowly look around the rooms and see if any of them are in darkness. If they are, ask for the light to gently penetrate that room and try to discern what is causing the darkness. Ask for the great love to shine all the way through, and breathe and rest in that love.

6. What Is Real?

All divine things gave me great pleasure; yet those of the world held me prisoner. I seem to have wanted to reconcile two opposites... the spiritual life and the joys, pleasures, and pastimes of the senses. (TL, 57)

TERESA STRUGGLED ENORMOUSLY with her dichotomous life, that is, with her desire for God on the one hand and her enjoyment of life's pleasures on the other. Teresa was not naive, however, and she was perfectly aware that God works in and through the world. It was the *attachment* to the ways of the world that concerned her, the desire for her senses to be satiated through the pleasures of personal attention and recognition. It was the subtlety of her pride and ego that she watched as they would rise again and again to receive praise and acknowledgment. Even though she was ostensibly doing God's work, she knew that she was erroneously claiming the credit.

Teresa instinctively knew that there was a greater purity to be had in living in this world, that there was a truth beyond personal and societal desires. In many Eastern traditions the ego and the world are understood as illusions; the reality is spirit, and all else is not real. Sometimes this philosophy can appear somewhat harsh, since it seems to dismiss as not real many of our painful earthly experiences. To me this speaks of separation — separating our ego-selves from our God-selves. But the ego is as much God as spirit is. To say that the ego is not God implies that it comes from elsewhere — but from where? All is God. If we try to deny the ego, it will only fight harder to survive. And if we look underneath all the desires and claims of the ego, we always come to the same conclusion: the ego is looking to be loved.

Teresa was known for her compassion and was always readily available to console and counsel any nuns, priests, or people in the community who were having difficulties. "Love one another," she would say. It is love that allows the ego to lie down calmly and to trust in the spirit of God working in our lives; it is love that shows us that the stories of the ego are not as enticing as we first thought.

When our ego rears its head with its demands, ideas, and get-rich schemes, we would do well first to send it love, and then to send it more love. When it is calm, check back in. Very often we will find that its impulsive ideas have completely dissolved. Sometimes this admonition to love, and especially to love others and their ideas, can seem overly demanding. Our reaction can be to run, since nobody enjoys being commanded to do anything, but is this not what many of the great prophets and religious figures have taught us? Yes, we are *commanded* to love. Assuring someone that she is loved allows her to return to the truth of her existence. This assurance can be given through a simple gesture or tender word. Truth without love can be harsh. Love without truth can fall into sentimentality. Together they work miracles, since they relate to our wholeness: our ego *and* our spirit.

Meditation

Letting yourself sink into a place of deep peace, breathe into the largeness of your spirit. Let yourself soak in the magnificent love that you are. Now invite your ego to join you, and allow it to be enveloped in this love. Hold the ego as you would a small child, and simply allow the love to permeate, no matter what arises. Just allow the love to flow.

7. Distracted Conversation

So, when I began to indulge in these conversations, seeing that they were customary, it did not seem to me that they would bring the harm and distraction to my soul that I afterwards found such behavior to entail. (TL, 52)

DURING TERESA'S EARLY YEARS in the Carmelite Convent it was common practice for the nuns to receive visitors. Owing to her father's wealth, Teresa had her own apartment in which she frequently entertained her friends and eagerly engaged in the worldly gossip that she still so dearly loved. Her life as a nun became perfunctory, since she attended required prayers but often did not actively participate. She noted how the conversations she indulged in distracted her from pursuing her spiritual life. Her mind became filled with details of society life, and her thoughts strayed to all kinds of desires and dreamed outcomes.

It was only through receiving a vision, in which she

was entreated to stop these interactions and told to listen to the voices of angels, that Teresa halted her participation in what she called "the ways of the world." She was being implored to make space for the voice of the divine to be heard and not to clutter her mind with worldly wishes and other desires that were not to her ultimate benefit.

How easy it is to become distracted! Very subtly we can hinder ourselves from the soul growth we are called to; our daily conversations are one such way for this to occur. Gossip, for Teresa, was a major component of distracted conversation. But what exactly is gossip, and how deeply does it affect who we are in our everyday lives?

The human psyche can be likened to a never-ending dramatic play, as the Greek playwrights and Shakespeare (among a few experts on human nature) have portrayed so well. In order for a drama to be successful there needs to be at least two characters, but preferably many more to provide a rich and varied story. The unfolding of our personal psychological history occurs as we move from being the protagonist to a minor character, from the victim to the perpetrator. This participation in our stories can become addictive; it is how many lead their lives. I would like to suggest trying a new role — that of lighting technician — placing light on situations arising and scenes being enacted, allowing for a different view of reality. How does this person look in this light? How do I look when I am saying these lines? Would another method of communication open this scene into a more loving dialogue? Is there truth to my words, or am I repeating secondhand information or socially dictated phrases?

Where there is truth and love the soul is nurtured — there is no need for stimulating the dramatic nature of the psyche. We no longer require other people's characters and stories, for there is no drama for them to act in. Concern for others becomes a real and loving experience. Too often we become caught in our own story or in the drama of others. By becoming the lighting technician we can effectively remove ourselves from the stage and see things in a different light.

Meditation

Sink slowly into your body, following the natural rhythm of your breath. Allow yourself to watch your conversations with others. Are they coming from a place of integrity and depth, or are they comments made automatically without thought? Are they calm and loving, or are they dramatic? There's no need to judge, only to watch. Now sink below the thoughts and conversations, reach into the place of love, and stay there.

8. The Mystery

*I can find nothing to compare with the great beauty
of a soul and its infinite capacity... the soul is nothing
but a paradise in which God takes delight. (IC, 28)*

TERESA WAS IN AWE OF THE SOUL. God had shown her that we are made in the image and likeness of our Creator, that is, we are all physical, emotional, and spiritual expressions of the divine nature. It is these expressions — what we can call our human and divine being — that give God great delight as He lovingly watches over our explorations and adventures.

Many have embarked on a soul exploration and are seeking the paradise that we have both descended from and are *heirs* to: the Garden of Eden. This place is the promise of a harmonious world and a state of peace and bliss, both within and without. It is both a memory and a hope. The Garden of Eden, however, is neither an external nor an internal place that we arrive at. Rather, it is an eternal journey into the mystery of who we are and who we are constantly becoming — it is not a destination.

This journey requires of us an expansiveness of spirit and mind, as we are given, at every moment, the opportunity to walk through the mind and soul of God. This is the "infinite capacity" that Teresa spoke of; there is no limit to what we can become. She also believed, however, that our reasoning minds, no matter how keen, can barely comprehend this awesomeness and can throw up enormous obstacles to entering this great mystery. Better that we not even try to use the mind, she suggested, since it has great difficulty grasping that we are magnificent souls who are one and the same as God.

Some physicists are beginning to comprehend the grandness of who we are and what we are a part of — this grand production called eternal life. Life does not stop moving and growing; it is in constant motion as it seeks to reproduce itself in the many varied and wonderful forms that make up our galaxies and those beyond.

All creation, from the minutest life form to the greatest mass, is a mystery and a grand miracle. Teresa believed that all things have their beneficial secrets and that the smallest creation, even an ant, contains more mysteries than we can understand. In our own selves there are great secrets that we do not know; and what we know of the universal mystery amounts to virtually nothing. Teresa invited us to expand into and to participate in this mystery; it is our divine right. In her deep understanding of this, she never tired of praising the magnificence of this eternal garden of which we are all caretakers — that is, our own souls.

We were born with great dignity and beauty. It is up to each of us to reclaim and live this infinitely sublime gift, with our humanity and divinity merging into this miracle of life. We, along with all life forms, are giving great delight to God right now, as we move and grow and change — just as a child gives joy to a parent. And just as the bond between child and parent is never severed, nothing can dissolve the eternal bond between a soul and God.

Meditation

Closing your eyes, gently allow yourself to fall into a place of deep rest. Ask to enter into a place of expansiveness; ask that the true nature of your soul come forward. See the great beauty and the infinite love that you are. Feel the mystery in and all around you. Breathe into who you are now — a wonderful and mysterious being.

9. Seeing Beyond the Veil

*As far as I can understand, the door of entry
into this castle is prayer and meditation . . . the soul is
advised to enter within itself. (IC, 31)*

WE ARE ALL SOULS with our own castles, but not all of
us may desire to move from the outer to the inner
court. Happy to remain on the outskirts, we do not
come to know the wonderful place or the riches that
wait for us on the inside. "Where their treasure is, there
is their heart also" (Matthew 6:21). Attached to our
preoccupations and worries, we live behind a veil of
ignorance about the truth of our being.

Teresa implored us to see beyond the veil and to
travel through all the royal rooms; the way of entry, she
found, was through prayer and meditation. In our
human evolutionary journey we have become too self-
reliant and too eager to claim credit for the things we

have achieved. What of divine assistance? What of divine law? We forget that beyond us is a universal force supplying life at every moment — with every breath we take, with every sun that rises and sets.

When we come to prayer with a humble heart, the door is opened much wider than when we think we are still affecting everything. Throughout her writings Teresa never tired of reminding us of the great benefits of entering into genuine humility, that is, of allowing the ego to release control. When we do this, our prayers can become pure and spontaneous thoughts of the soul, or simply a state of being where we rest rather than constant petitions for what we want.

Teresa strongly disliked repetitive prayers and voiced her displeasure at this religious ritual: "Would we give a friend so little attention?" she asked. She actively encouraged praying with thought and feeling and demanded respectful interaction with the divine, not simply uttering words out of habit or hope. She also introduced the practice of meditation to the Carmelite Order and was considered an expert on this subject, which her numerous writings attest to.

Believing herself incapable of meditation, after many attempts, Teresa (temporarily) gave up the practice. She warned against such nonsense and called for perseverance, saying that we need to release any expectation of what we think should happen and to rely on God to guide us. There are many rooms in the castle, she reminded us, and we may be taken to any of these rooms at any time — it is not up to us to decide where we need to go. Our meditations and prayers can take us into places of deep peace, or into longing and pain; unbidden memories may surface, or feelings of lightness and grace may pervade our soul. As we journey toward the center of our being, may we be open to visiting all the rooms in our castle.

Meditation

Relax into the quietness of your being. Lay down your need to control, and agree to let the divine guide you. Breathe, and trust that you will be taken where you need to go. Breathe deeper and deeper into your being — let yourself go to wherever you are being taken.

Second Dwelling

THE RETURN

A soul can perform many acts to confirm its resolution to serve God, and to awaken love in itself. (TL, 84)

In moments of awakening we are given the eyes of God with which to see the other, grander reality of our lives. These moments are also invitations to return to God and to ourselves. The original meaning of the word *religion* was "to return," and by this act of returning we reignite the divine spark that resides within.

According to Teresa, in this second dwelling we must become active and help God to light the fire of love within our hearts. We must commit to our spiritual journey and spend time building our relationship with the inner divine self. In so doing, we will also meet, again and again, the voice of our ego. Teresa tells us how to discern the voices we hear, enabling us to have confidence in knowing the voice of God and allaying our doubt and confusion.

10. My Time

*Even when we are engaged in our worldly pastimes,
businesses and pleasures and haggling... this God of ours is
so anxious that we should desire Him and strive after His
companionship that He calls us ceaselessly, time after time to
approach Him; and this voice of His is so sweet. (IC, 47)*

ENTERING THE CASTLE requires a commitment, and as
Teresa believed, we need to make an effort to remain
within its walls. Upon entering the castle and moving
closer to where God resides, our inner hearing
becomes more attuned to His voice. He is a very good
neighbor, said Teresa, one who is very generous with
His love and who never tires of calling us to come
closer, even through the noise and commotion of our
daily life.

God is committed to us, to the purity of a loving
relationship. Are we committed to the same? Teresa
believed that the desire to commit is essential, enabling
this relationship to grow and facilitating our ability to

know and love ourselves. We must create the sacred time and space to be fully present with ourselves and with God. In this way we can be open to the inner workings of our soul, and we can develop a more astute ability to hear God speaking in us and through us.

With our very busy lives, it may sometimes seem impossible to have such a luxury as time for ourselves. And when time does become available, it is very often accompanied by sheer exhaustion from the day's activities. However, Teresa was not asking us to fit God into our schedule — she was telling us to make this relationship a priority. This relationship is the very cornerstone of our life. Often we are too busy "doing" our life, rather than cultivating the being that we are.

"His voice is so sweet," wrote Teresa. Have we heard the sweetness and felt the gentleness that this great love brings? Or have we rushed by it in our attempt to have a few minutes to ourselves at the end of the day? God is extremely patient and will wait for you. You do not need to rush anywhere or be anything; just come as you are, even in your frazzled state, but be committed to spending time. Be committed to coming openly and honestly as you would to a dear friend. Create a time in the day or evening, even just five or ten minutes, that is just for you and your divine self. You will come to enjoy these private and sacred moments, and they will naturally grow longer.

This is a commitment to *you,* to coming to know yourself in ways previously unexplored. See it as a soulful adventure, an exploration into the wonder of what it is to be a human being on this earth. This is not something you have to do to improve your life. There is no aim, only a commitment to be exactly who you are. This is the richness of entering the castle.

Teresa led an extraordinarily busy life as founder of the new Carmelite Order. She dealt with financial and administrative duties, oversaw daily monastic activities, gave spiritual counseling, and wrote prolifically. She complained about the volume of her duties, and she desired to be left alone to her prayer time — this was the most precious thing for her. Without it, she said, she would have been unable to achieve anything.

Commit yourself to God, she said, and your life will naturally unfold.

Meditation

Create a sacred and quiet place. Let yourself be guided into your inner castle, and feel the ease and peace to be had there. See yourself exactly as you are. Do not judge or change anything. Allow yourself to be. Commit to that self. Ask that you may hear the sweetness of God's voice. Let it radiate through your whole being. Commit to that voice.

11. Conversing with God

*[God] knows best what is suitable for us. There's no need
for us to be advising Him about what He should give
us... to bring your will into conformity with God's will
... the greatest perfection attainable along the spiritual path
lies in this conformity. (CW vol. II, 301)*

THE PRAYER OF PETITION, or our contemporary spiritual equivalent, "manifestation," may originate from the same source, that is, from our own will and desire. Teresa believed this to be a common error that many people make as they walk the spiritual path. Essentially, she said, we are attempting to make God bend to our will and deliver what *we* want. Everyone beginning a life of prayer and meditation, she said, should be determined for the human and divine will to become aligned. For Teresa, this determination occurred many times throughout the day and throughout her life, as she asked, "Your will be done and not mine."

Our minds are filled with many thoughts and

wishes of what we think should occur in our lives. Very often these are the dreams of the ego that have slowly accumulated through societal influences, peer and family suggestions, and unfulfilled needs of love and attention. If we are able to remove these external layers we will find our true nature waiting to bloom. In living from this true nature, we will be given more than we could even think to desire.

For Teresa, it was turning to her inner God that freed her of societal expectations and her past soul wounds. She believed that at times we need to pour out our souls to God, just as we would to a friend, knowing that the power of love can dissolve anything that may be hindering our progress. All we need to do is bring our desire to heal. However, we must also be open and not try to dictate what we think should happen. Sometimes, Teresa said, God allows certain occurrences, even perhaps painful ones, that we would not willingly choose so that we may learn and grow.

Surrender is the key word, easy to say but far more difficult to live. We wrestle with God at every moment that we resist what is happening in our lives. For Teresa, surrender was a lifelong project; at no point should we become discouraged. Even when we fall back into our own will, God can also use this for our benefit.

Who are we to advise God of what we need? God already knows our needs and is waiting anxiously to meet them. The ego, however, will take us on many detours, and we will expend a lot of energy as we try to make things happen in accordance with its desires.

By aligning our will to our inner God-self we can travel much more quickly and easily to a life of fulfillment. Teresa wrote, "It is the person who lives in more perfect conformity who will receive more...and be more advanced on this road" (*CW* vol. II, 301).

Meditation

Let yourself fall gently into the breath. Allow all your desires and wishes to surface — let them speak to you of their longing — and hear what they have to say. Now hold them in the great love of your God-self — let them be loved. Allow yourself to be guided to wherever you need to go, and surrender into the love that is taking you.

12. Hearing the Voice of God

*Consider the words that the divine mouth speaks,
for in the first word you will understand immediately the
love He has for you. (CW vol. II, 137)*

OUR SOULS HAVE BEEN WANDERING for many years at their own pleasure, said Teresa, or more accurately, in their own grief. Unaccustomed to hearing the divine words of love, we need to learn to recognize them and to openly invite them to once more reside within. This kind of inspiration can come from both external and internal sources. God is all around us and within us, and His desire to communicate with us is quietly waiting to be fulfilled.

How do we know when we are hearing the voice of God, and how do we distinguish between it and our own voice of desire? Teresa believed that as we spend more time within our interior castle, we will come to discern the words meant for our benefit, that we will eventually come to know the voice that brings the sweetest of all love. She does, however, provide us with some clear guidelines to help us while we are developing this gift of discernment.

While we are meditating it is common for words or messages to be conveyed and if, Teresa said, we have no doubts and there is complete clarity and certainty within the soul, then we can be confident that we are hearing the divine voice. If it is our own wishes and desires being expressed, the words will be less clear, even appearing somewhat murky, causing confusion to our souls. Very often things will come as a complete surprise, perhaps something that you would not normally entertain or even desire — this too can be a generous nudge from God.

Sometimes ideas and instructions can be conveyed in their entirety in what appears to be only a moment, and we can fully grasp and understand them. Perhaps this best describes the flash of creative genius as a problem is understood, a theorem developed, or a piece of music heard and then composed in its entirety. Those who have received such a gift know it to be the work of divine inspiration.

When there is a feeling of peace and lightness in the soul, wrote Teresa, this is a very good indication that we have received divine words of love. If the soul is restless or our thoughts are in turmoil, this can be understood to be the workings of the ego and the mind. And last, if we are able to transcend the self and become more concerned with honoring the great mystery of God, this is the divine not only speaking to us but also making itself at home in our souls.

Our external world also provides many avenues for God to work through, if we are open to receive the gifts from our fellow beings and from the life all around us. When we are open to receive and when we remove all judgment, anyone and anything can be our divine messenger. It can be a homeless person on the street, a flower blossoming in our garden, the presence of a bird, or a dear friend with loving arms — in other words, all of life. Learning to hear and discern the divine words, in both our external and internal worlds, makes for a very rich and fulfilled life.

Meditation

Closing your eyes and resting the mind, allow all the internal voices to come into silence by gently placing them in love. Invite the divine words into your castle, into your internal home — allow them to come in their own way and their own time. Feel the external world around you and open yourself to its love. Gently relax into the love within you and all around you, and receive.

13. Inclined to Love

The will is inclined to love after seeing such countless signs of love . . . it especially keeps in mind how this true Lover never leaves it, accompanying it and giving it life and being. (CW vol. II, 299)

AS WE EXPERIENCE and become more receptive to the divine love available to us, our souls slowly begin to understand that we are sincerely loved. This may, however, be a long process, since the faculties of the mind, including our memory, are continually providing us with examples of when we have not felt loved. Sometimes it appears that this is their sole purpose — to remind us of such occasions. This is when we can employ the will, said Teresa, allowing it to work for the good of our soul.

If we find ourselves overwhelmed with sadness, because we do not feel loved by or connected to others, we can decide to look at all the ways that love *is* present in our lives. If it is not the right time to be with others, perhaps nature will provide the desired connection. Teresa was a great lover of roses. As a young girl her favorite place at home was the garden, and this love continued throughout her life; she frequently would be seen wandering alone in prayerful thought through the monastic gardens.

We can also train our memory to remind us of the times when we have experienced love. The memory is quick to bring forward times of disappointment, so let it become equally adept at relaying cherished moments. Let us remember the friendship and love we have received, and let us look at how they occurred. Usually they required nothing more than our openness — our willingness to receive — and the ability to be ourselves, with all our vulnerabilities. In sinking into our sadness we can close down to loving opportunities, and perhaps all we need do is share the fragile feeling openly with another in order to feel loved again.

We need, in these down times, to be reminded of who resides within — the purity of love itself. We may not *feel* the love, but it becomes an act of will to acknowledge the reality of this truth. Teresa believed that no greater friend can be found than the one who lives deep within our soul. If we grow accustomed to this presence, she said, "we will not be able to get away" (*CW* vol. II, 133), and we will find this presence everywhere. In time, even sadness will melt into the great love.

Teresa believed that the soul, when open, becomes

enkindled in love, and it doesn't understand how it is happening. It knows that it enjoys this love, and that clearly the joy is not coming through the satisfaction of the intellect or the fulfillment of a desire. The will also becomes enkindled with this love, without understanding how. It is, Teresa said, a gift from the divine — a gift to use for the growth of our soul and for the benefit of others, as we walk in a blind world that does not always see the abundance of love available everywhere.

Meditation

Falling into the gentleness of your breath, allow the divine friend to be with you. Let this friend give to you all that He desires — allow your soul to be open to receive. Let any sadness, grief, or loneliness be washed clean in the love. Allow yourself to melt into the divine arms.

14. The Castle of Peace

*Outside this castle neither security nor peace
will be found . . . [the soul] should avoid going
about to strange houses since its own is so
filled with blessings. (CW vol. II, 299)*

TERESA PRAYED FOR SOULS returning to the castle
that they not be deceived by a false sense of peace and
security in the material benefits of the world. She asked
for these souls to be enlightened so that they would
not give up what they had begun but would continue
to know that good lay within. She noted that as we
walk the spiritual path, our lives continue as before —
bringing daily blessings and trials. What matters is how
we respond to the circumstances placed before us.

There are many kinds of peace, and just as many
opportunities to experience its absence. For Teresa the
attitude of lack was perhaps the most basic example of
this absence of peace. She would chide her nuns for

their lack of trust when it came to having food, money, or clothing supplied. She would also teach them, however, that to go without these things for a short time was not something to become disturbed about. She did not adhere to a life of asceticism, but she believed in the benefit of self-control so as not to become a slave to the desires of the body. We should maintain our peace, she said, whether we are experiencing abundance or lack.

Teresa believed that regardless of our financial status, we all have a responsibility not to become attached to the great power money can wield over us — rich and poor alike. By releasing this attachment, the rich can use their funds for the betterment of all our brothers and sisters, and the poor can be open to receiving God's abundance in all its forms.

Teresa found life's upsets, such as family illness and death, personally difficult. She was an extremely passionate woman with strong emotional ties to her family, and when her father became seriously ill she left the convent to go care for him. She described how distressing this was to her and how in losing him she was losing all her comfort in life. When he passed from this life, she said, "I felt as if my soul were being torn from my body" (*TL,* 56). It was only by surrendering her emotions to God that she once more regained her inner peace.

Too often we become disillusioned by believing that peace will be ours when we are intimately involved with another. We may certainly feel a calm in the presence of another; however, it will only be temporary unless we can also maintain that internal state of being. Teresa believed that we rush here and there looking for this peace, and yet we have everything we need, right here in our own homes. Through this very act of searching outside ourselves, we acknowledge that we do not have the ability to create our own peace. As we search, and do not find, we experience dissatisfaction and disappointment. Peace becomes something we elusively pursue rather than something we know to be within us.

"Peace I bring to you, My own peace I give to you" (John 14:27). These are the words Jesus spoke to His disciples. What is this peace he brings, asked Teresa? It is the knowledge that we, like Jesus, have an innately divine nature, and that we have the ability to see into and through our humanity. That is, we live in the world but are not of the world. Peace belongs to us as we belong to it; it is ours to eternally abide in.

Meditation

Falling within yourself, feel the deep internal peace that is innately yours. Allow the whole of your being to contain this peace. Know that it is completely yours. Now begin to breathe this peace around you. This is who you are, living in the world.

15. Know Thy Self

*Knowing ourselves is something so important that I
wouldn't want any relaxation ever in this regard . . . it is
good, indeed very good, to try to enter first into the room
where self-knowledge is dealt with. (CW vol. II, 292)*

THROUGHOUT HER LIFE, Teresa stressed the importance of beginning the journey of self-knowledge.
This journey requires an ability to be very honest with
oneself and a desire for self-responsibility. It means that
we no longer blame others for the state of our soul, or
project our old wounds onto new (or old) friends. It
means we are able to acknowledge to ourselves, and
speak clearly to others, the thoughts and emotions we
are experiencing. We can become too easily distracted
by higher spiritual truths and teachings and neglect to
look at the way we live in this world — as psychological and physical beings.

We are a grand mixture of ancestral, genetic, psychological, and spiritual components. All these come to light in our daily lives, and many of them are not as attractive as we would desire. Teresa reminded us that by acknowledging these not-so-welcome traits, we are entering into the realm of humility — the place where we understand that we are superior to none, the place we can all afford to dwell in. Our ego would of course prefer not to enter this room, and our pride struggles to remind us that we *are* better than others. It does not want to face those darker areas of our personality.

The trickster resides within us all and will certainly emerge whenever we bring light into the darkness. It will try to divert our attention or explain and defend its position. We may find ourselves suddenly becoming preoccupied with a phone call we have to make or an email we have to send. Or we could find ourselves embroiled in a very complex inner dialogue as we comb previous situations for minute details, our every word justified and our position defended. When we find ourselves falling into the traps of the trickster, Teresa advised us to bring ourselves lovingly back into the presence of the One who knows and to place ourselves humbly at His feet. Through this action we acknowledge that it is this loving One who sheds the light into our hearts, not the ego. Only then will the truth of our self be revealed.

This journey of knowing the self is a constant process

— we move in and out of the room of self-knowledge as our life and soul demand. Teresa draws an analogy with a bee making honey in a hive: the bee is always working to make the honey, but sometimes it leaves the beehive and flies about gathering nectar from the flowers. Similarly, she said, the soul needs to fly into other realms to experience the nectar of God, to not always concentrate on the earthly self.

For Teresa, self-knowledge and humility are the two greatest attributes we can bring to our spiritual life — whatever stage we may be at. Those most advanced know that visiting these dwellings brings them closer to God, and so they take great delight when they are guided there.

Meditation

Feel yourself relaxing into the breath. Open your heart and soul, and feel safe doing so. Ask for something of yourself to be revealed. Receive it with love, knowing it is a part of you. See how it affects you daily, and take this new awareness into your life.

16. False Humility

If we are always fixed on our earthly misery,
the stream will never flow free from the mud of fears...
souls think that all such fears stem from humility...
we never get free from ourselves. (CW vol. II, 292–93)

TERESA BELIEVED THAT IT IS VERY EASY to fall into a kind of false humility by thinking we are not good enough to receive God's many wonderful graces. Humility is not achieved by refusing the generosity of the divine but rather by accepting and understanding the generous nature always available to us and by taking delight in the sacred gifts. How can we ignore such abundance? Why do we choose to remain poor of spirit instead of reveling in our true nature?

As we journey into self-knowledge, we may sometimes come to have a distorted image of who we are; our very earnestness to discover the self can in fact become a hindrance. This is evident when we become overly concerned about ourselves: we look to see whether or not others are watching us and tailor our actions according to what would be considered humble and spiritual; we spend excessive amounts of time trying to decide if a particular path would be beneficial for us; we wonder if others will judge us or think that we believe ourselves to be superior if we do not follow their path.

We may consider these thoughts to be humble, but in fact, said Teresa, they are fears that arise from a misunderstanding of self-knowledge, and they all evolve from the same place — a feeling of spiritual inferiority. Since true spirit does not know either superiority or inferiority, we are clearly dealing with the workings of the ego, which firmly believes that it is engaging in the spiritual life. Teresa lamented this illusory belief and saw many souls living this falsity.

Similarly, this belief is also evident in our conversations. How easy it is to fall into spiritual talk and platitudes, repeating teachings without thought or belief, without knowledge or committed experience. We fall into spiritual trends that change as quickly as new teachers emerge — we replace one with another, always seeking new methods of enlightenment. This dynamic too can be viewed as a false humility, since our continual search means that we do not feel good enough or *healed* enough to enter the Kingdom of God.

Ironically, we are the very place that we have to enter, we *are* the very place that we are looking for, and we *are* good enough to make our way home. Do not allow, said Teresa, any erroneous idea of humility to stop you from coming to know the One who lives within. Such a good Guest should not be turned away. Let us come forward and greet Him as He deserves, and as we deserve.

So when we feel ourselves shrinking inward, or perhaps when we hear our inner voice saying, "Who am I to think/receive such a thing" or "I am not good enough," then let us step outward and say, "Yes, this is who I am." And let us be grateful for what we are receiving and for the ability to take a step closer to who we are.

Meditation

Feel yourself coming into a gentle place of rest. Allow any feeling of unworthiness to rise. Ask God to love those feelings and the part of you they arose from. Feel the desire to let them go, and let them dissolve into love. Feel your own goodness, and know that you are perfect just as you are.

17. The Doubting Mind

It is in this stage that the worldly things and temporal pleasures are represented as though almost eternal . . . the poor soul, how distressed it is, not knowing if it should proceed further or return to the room where it was before! (IC, 48)

UPON MAKING THE RETURN JOURNEY TO GOD, we are lovingly seduced into the new life we are being given. There comes a time, however, when doubts rise to assault us. They remind us of where we have come from — the world with its own rules, with its infinite games of power, wealth, and stature. We are blatantly shown how we are no longer involved in this game, and as a consequence we feel that we have lost something of value. A seed of doubt is sown, and our mind quickly waters this seed to exaggerate this feeling of loss. We so easily forget what we have gained.

As we voice our new understanding of the world to family, friends, and colleagues, we may be met with derision and disbelief, and their doubts about our chosen pathway can become a catalyst for our own. Our previous strength and conviction can begin to crumble as we entertain the thoughts of others. We question our real motives, and very often, our sanity. We begin to wonder if what we have been experiencing is real; maybe it has been an illusion? Maybe it has all been a construct of our imagination? The soul falls into very deep confusion.

As a consequence, our professional and personal esteem can be seriously affected, and very often we become isolated, as we begin to doubt both our spiritual choices and our old ways in the world. There is no refuge in either. The soul does not know where it should be residing, or in which direction it should be traveling.

Teresa believed this to be a time of great trial for the soul, one she was only too familiar with as she began down her chosen path. Suddenly our spiritual insight is lost, and all that we can see before us are the things of the world that give us pleasure. We become consumed by our desires and want to run toward them, believing them to be the true fulfillment of our life. Reason then joins in to validate this belief, she said, reminding us of the "eternal happiness" of those living such lives. We deliberately overlook the misfortunes that also assail them.

The mind becomes frenzied, as the need for personal power and control join to do battle with the spirit. Teresa cried out to God, "Ah, my Lord! Your

help is necessary here; without it one can do nothing...do not allow this soul to be deluded when its
journey has only begun" (*CW* vol. II, 300).

In many ways we all begin our journey over and
over again. As we travel on our path, we are confronted
with numerous desires still exerting power over us,
including the desire for power itself. The force of these
desires can enter all areas of our life — our work and
our personal relationships — and it can show up as an
addiction to a substance or to a state of mind. We are
not free if we are wielding power over someone, or if
we are under the powerful influence of another or of
our own dominating and doubtful thoughts. Let us be
like Teresa and cry out to our God, asking for our
doubts to be removed and for our desires to be in
accordance with the growth of our soul.

Meditation

*Feeling the gentleness of your breath, let yourself travel deeply
within. Relax there. When you are ready, allow any doubts
about your spiritual life to arise. Then ask God to let you see
them in their reality. Bless them and let them go. Ask that
your desires be for your highest good.*

18. Accepting God's Advice

*One must not think of such things as spiritual favors,
for that is a very poor way of starting to build
such a precious and great edifice. (IC, 50)*

IT IS EASY TO BECOME LURED into spiritual sensationalism, that is, expecting to have experiences that make us feel especially connected to God. While we pray and meditate we may see, hear, or feel the divine presence in many ways. However, it is also possible, and often very likely, that we will not experience the divine in any form. The soul may feel, as a result of this lack of experience, that it is not making the desired connection and therefore that something is wrong. We can then become overly concerned about the nature of spiritual experience and seek ways to further enhance spiritual pleasure rather than simply allowing the spirit of God to guide us.

These times of "dryness," wrote Teresa, are given to us by God so that we may become more spiritually mature. Just as a baby first crawls and then gradually learns to walk, so too must we learn to take our own first spiritual steps. But we must also note that they may not always be in the direction that we would like to take, and we may not always agree with God's methods. As we are walking in this unwelcome dryness we may witness others being given all sorts of spiritual gifts. Teresa says we are to "blindfold the eyes of the mind" (*TL*, 81) so as not to compare our journey with theirs. And she asked what difference it should make to us what others are or are not receiving. Who are we to question the workings of God and of other souls?

Under no circumstances, said Teresa, are we to give up our time of prayer and meditation, no matter how tedious it becomes; this would be like saying that since we are no longer receiving anything we will not spend our time this way. Can you imagine acting like this with our friends and lovers? What if, in a moment of not receiving anything from them, we ceased spending time with them?

The small amount of time we do spend in prayer and meditation, Teresa believed, should be given wholly to God — we should consider it not ours but His. And we should become determined never to take it back — not for any trial or challenge we experience, not for any contradiction in our life, not for any dryness we experience in prayer. Ultimately, what Teresa is saying is that no matter what is occurring in our life, we are not to abandon the relationship that is the very core of our existence.

Living in the love of God does not always mean being bathed in delight and tenderness (even though this is what we would all prefer). What it does mean is serving the divine relationship with fortitude and humility. When things in our life become less than pleasurable, naturally we want them to become easier. Teresa ascertained, however, that such a desire lacks the freedom our spirit requires. The spirit needs to roam where it is guided, and we can join in this courageous adventure by allowing it to accomplish what it is here to do.

Meditation

Coming into your quiet place of being, bring yourself fully into the presence of God, not expecting anything, only coming to give — of yourself and your time. Give freely, and allow yourself to simply be with He who loves you. Let your spirit roam where it needs to — let your courage emerge to help you. Bless your life for all that it is.

Third Dwelling

SELF-KNOWLEDGE

For with these fears, what happiness can anyone have?
(CW vol. II, 305)

The third dwelling is where we reside most of the time. Our fears and worries take precedence, and we are either unwilling or unable to release control of our existence to the greater benevolence of God's care. Why is this so?

In this dwelling we begin to experience the spiritual truths influencing our everyday lives; old theories and paradigms become dismantled, and we are asked to look honestly at ourselves and to discover where our true security lies. Is it in God, or is it in our material life that we have so carefully constructed? The path of self-knowledge can at times be painful, but Teresa assured us that with perseverance and the ability to acknowledge our own truth, we will be richly rewarded.

19. Handing Over Your Life

We all say we desire it; but if God is to take complete possession of the soul, more than that is necessary. Words are not enough. (IC, 59)

HOW EASY IT IS TO DECLARE TO GOD, in the heat of spiritual love and fervor, that we wish to give ourselves to the light of divine love. Our desire is so strong, since we innately know that this giving of ourselves is the way to truthful living. God, of course, takes our words seriously and immediately comes to claim us. In the process, all sorts of psychological and spiritual dross may be revealed, and the process of purification begins. At this point our lives may be turned completely around, with our work, relationships, and cherished beliefs slowly, or quickly, becoming dismantled.

Was this what we had in mind when we declared our love? Probably it was not. We may then enter a phase of controlled panic, as somewhere deep within we know that what is occurring is for our own good. Yet we are also seriously questioning the bedlam that our life has become. We may experience extreme discomfort, with conversations and relationships no longer providing the consolation that we had grown accustomed to. We question our beliefs and ideologies, and what may have previously been a resting place for us now becomes dismantled. We are left wandering in the rubble trying to salvage any shred of belief that we once had. What began as a declaration of love seems to have rapidly declined into a place of confusion and unrest.

At this point, we may try to take back our words and undo our consequent actions, and of course, the choice is ours. To be possessed by God, said Teresa, is no small matter. But if we think that it is we who must navigate our way through the rubble, then it would be natural for us to opt for the quickest and easiest route out. Yet in allowing God to be the navigator, we can relax and become a witness to all that is occurring. This relaxation in itself is an art form to be studied, and we are all enrolled as lifelong students; the more willing we are to loosen control over our lives, the easier both the relaxation and the living become.

Our spiritual lives demand more from us than we expect; as we take one step, the next is already inviting us forward. This need not be a painful process, even though many of us have experienced it that way. Find the joy, said Teresa, in coming before the One whom you love, and allow Him to guide you in the way that is for your greater good. This becomes easier as the soul witnesses the freedom and love that follow each new step we take. Learn to take delight in this birthing process. When we come to truly understand to *whom* we are giving birth, the pain will disappear.

When we come before God with words of love declared, we are giving ourselves permission to be transformed. Let us come with a joyful heart, knowing that we are starting a journey that our minds cannot even imagine and our imaginations cannot yet see.

Meditation

Allow yourself to be enveloped by the love within and all around you. Know that you are constantly giving birth to the divine love within you — feel any pain in this birthing and feel it subside. Allow the tears of love to flow; ask that you may feel the joy of this constant new love; breathe into this joy and know that it is yours.

20. Security in God

It really is a great misery to be alive when we have always to be going about like those with enemies at their gates, who cannot lay aside their arms even when sleeping or eating, and are always afraid of being surprised by a breaching of their fortress in some weak spot. (IC, 56)

THROUGHOUT OUR LIVES, many of us succeed in building a strong fortress around our souls for protection. We have taken up the position of guard, always alert to some intruder who may not be welcome or who may pose a threat to our safety. We have also set a king or queen on a throne to make decisions and rules so that our lives may run smoothly and so that we may feel secure. We are the mistress or master of our own kingdom and take refuge in what we have created.

What a lot of work we have made for ourselves! And, as many of us discover, this fortress is not really as secure as we would like it to be. God will always find the weak spots within our walls, and He will relentlessly send His messengers to help deliver us from our illusion of false security. These messengers may take the form of a lover coming to help reveal the tenderness of our heart, a teacher reminding us that it is God who reigns within, or maybe a child to disrupt our orderly lives, bringing love back into the chaos of our life. We so easily imprison our lives in an inflexible structure, expending so much energy in keeping love *out,* saying, "No, God, thank you, but I do not need your help."

And yet, as Teresa tells us, the soul becomes so tired when we live this way. We take responsibility for *everything* and do not allow the spirit of God to guide us with ease and grace. We create so much work for ourselves, and gradually this wonder called life becomes nothing more than a trudging through time. There is very little enthusiasm or energy available to us for truly living and loving. It is time for our internal king or queen to abdicate and to deliver the rulership to the divine. It is also time to call in the sentries and allow them to relax their guard duties — with the divine in the holy seat of guidance, we can trust that only friends bearing gifts for our greater good will be visiting.

Teresa believed that it is no wonder we have difficulty trusting, when for so long the smaller ego-self has been offering advice and making the decisions, which at the best of times is questionable, if not comical. Teresa often remarked on how amusing she found herself as she watched her ego trying to convince her of all sorts of ridiculous notions. We must come to know these voices, she said, *and they are many,* waiting to take us down a road of fear, insecurity, and at times para-noia. They will tell you to reinforce the walls of your fortress and to employ more guards, but in coming to recognize these voices, we can hand them over to our inner reigning God.

In time we will learn to trust in God's wisdom and love and come to know that this is where our ultimate security lies. We will move from the walled fortress into the luminous castle, where our true selves and ever-abiding love reside.

Meditation

Feel yourself merging into the breath of silence. Become aware of the cracks in your fortress walls — feel what and who they are — and then gently let the wall crumble. Ask the divine presence to come forward and to let your walls be made of light. Let the love shine through the whole castle.

21. Spiritual Perseverance

One always gains much through perseverance...
[God] gives to each person a proper task, one that
He sees as appropriate for that person's soul... if you
have done what you can to be prepared, do not fear
that your effort will be lost. (CW vol. II, 103)

SOMETIMES IT FEELS THAT OUR ENDEAVORS are wasted. We do not always see the benefit in following what we believe to be the best possible path for ourselves. At times it can even feel as if we are being persecuted for the virtuous choices we have made. Bitterness can then arise in our souls as we struggle through, grumbling to God about the state of our lives. The joy we previously experienced in awakening and returning to ourselves can suddenly seem like a tedious job, making the soul feel dull, flat, and tired.

Teresa warned about this state of being, saying that souls who find themselves in this place need to quickly reassess their belief structure, since they are falling prey to an illusion that is harmful to their soul growth. God does not intend for us to struggle, to feel trapped, or to play the role of a martyr. If we are suffering in these ways, we are deluding ourselves that what we are doing is for God or for our own growth. For instance, we may find ourselves in a relationship that has become full of conflict, with one or both parties frequently feeling dishonored and disrespected. We continue, however, to remain in the relationship, since we feel it is *good* for us and that we are learning valuable lessons. This may even be the case, if it occurs infrequently, but very often it becomes an insidious pattern that we sadly not only become accustomed to but also come to expect. God does not want this for us.

Likewise, we may find ourselves staying in a job that is not suitable to the makeup of our soul. But since many of us have grown up with a strict work ethic, we may remain in this position. In the narrowness of our vision we do not see an alternative. We then begin a process of spiritual rationalization. This is when we find all sorts of reasons why God wants us to remain where we are. Meanwhile, the soul is dying. God does not want this either.

Self-imposed suffering is a common occurrence in our world. Teresa found this to be an anathema and sought compassion as the cure. We cannot fight reason with reason, she said; we can only fall into the realm of compassion — that deep place of understanding and love — for ourselves and for others. We need to awaken to the truth that God is on our side and that our spiritual lessons are not learned with a heaviness of soul but with a lightness of being. By becoming aware of these soul feelings we are able to discern between our self-imposed beliefs about growth and the true divine lessons.

Our perseverance with our spiritual growth can be a joy; it need not be a feeling of drudgery. We can bless and thank God, rather than complaining and grumbling. Our lessons can be learned with ease and gratitude, and we can begin to enjoy life once more, as was intended by the divine Creator.

Meditation

Begin by blessing your life and all that it holds — then let yourself gently slip into the arms of God. Feel any struggle in your life, any place where you may feel trapped. Offer these situations to God and ask that He breathe His blessing upon them. Allow His love to show you the truth, and ask to be guided into the gentleness and joy of your growth.

22. Love Has No Reason

Avoid tiring yourselves or wasting your thoughts in subtle reasoning about what you cannot properly understand. . . . When His Majesty desires to give understanding, He does so without our effort. (CW vol. II, 216)

HUMANITY IS STILL EMERGING from an era of obsession with reason and meaning, with seeking an answer to the perennial question: why did this happen? The human psyche possesses an innate curiosity that makes it very difficult for us to simply accept what has occurred without an explanation. We are obsessed with knowing and understanding — from the minutest details in our lives to the greatest universal mysteries.

If something goes wrong, we immediately search for the reason why. Numerous scenarios can then follow: we could blame ourselves and subsequently fall into guilt; we could revisit details of the situation again and again, with the mind each time providing a new set of reasons, ending in confusion and mental exhaustion; or we could understand it to be a karmic punishment for our past deeds.

If something goes right in our lives we tend to search for confirmation of our dreams and wishes, that is, for the spiritual meaning behind the occurrence. Perhaps we desire to meet our loved one. Too often a synchronistic meeting will immediately be understood as that *very one* arriving at the door of our heart. Perhaps this person is meant as a friend only. However, since we have already formulated our conclusion, imbuing it with spiritual meaning, we embark on an erroneous path, and ultimately we are disappointed.

If we are living this way, said Teresa, "Love has not yet reached the point of overwhelming reason" (*CW* vol. II, 312). Consequently, we continue to live a small and repetitive existence, as we bind and categorize our world into circumstances of spiritual reasoning and meaning. Teresa came to delight in not knowing the reasons for things occurring in her life, understanding that in doing so she was entering into a mystery far greater than anything her mind could comprehend. She believed that we must empty ourselves of the incessant need to know with our intellectual faculties *only*. We are being invited to begin knowing and understanding from a more spacious plane of existence — the soul — which contains *all* faculties in equilibrium. Teresa said to make no mistake about the spaciousness of our soul, which she believed to be capable of much more than we can imagine.

There are two types of acceptance. One is passive and fatalistic by nature, whereby we merely accept things without room for change or growth. This is the realm of the helpless victim. The other kind is active and open and comes through a personal willingness to accept only those things that are good for the soul. By accepting only the latter situations in our lives we are surrendering to love in all its grandness. In ceasing to manipulate this love, that is, by no longer trying to adapt it to our beliefs and desires, we begin to participate in the great mystery of the universe — that is, in God.

Meditation

Allow yourself to enter a place of silence and space. Breathe into the mystery that is contained in this vastness of love — let it penetrate in and through all that you are. Allow the smallness of your mind to be engulfed, and let the soul expand. Say yes to the mystery and all that it brings to your life.

23. Fear and Worry

*Let us leave our fears in His hands and let us forget
the weakness of our nature which is apt to cause
us so much worry. (IC, 66)*

OUR FEAR AND WORRIES BEGIN in our imaginations.
First, we think about and see obstacles, real or imag-
ined, before us. These thoughts and images then promote fear, which ripples through the body. Next, we
start to worry, as we imagine *all* the possible outcomes
that could occur and try to think of ways to prevent
their happening. We become victims of fearful thought,
and it continues to grow until we are able to release
ourselves from its grip. But what is this fear, and why
does it have such a strong hold over us?

Fear is an acknowledgment that we are entering a
realm that we have no control over; it is a place we are
unfamiliar with and do not know how to effectively

handle. Since we are creatures of control, this is an extremely uncomfortable predicament, so fear is born.

Teresa experienced enormous fear in the first half of her life as a nun. It was standard practice for the nuns to speak about the nature of their prayer life and the inner state of their soul to a priest. Their relationship with God was to be revealed as accurately and honestly as possible, which of course Teresa complied with. Owing to the intense and intimate degree of her relationship with the divine, the priests often told Teresa that she was being misled. She was told that her experiences did not issue from God at all. It was the devil, they said, and she was ordered to rebuke all such experiences. But apparently God did not agree, and He did not cease in communicating with Teresa through ecstatic means. He did this by absorbing her in divine love, whereby she entered altered states of being. These experiences lasted anywhere from a minute to several hours.

Teresa worried incessantly that her soul was in danger, and she spent many hours fretting that her life was nothing but an illusion. All that was occurring, of course, was that she was walking an unfamiliar path. The priests, not having experienced these prayerful ecstasies of absorption, could not imagine that God would speak to a soul in such a way. In fact, many of them had not truly heard, or had ceased hearing, the voice of God. This was the conclusion that Teresa finally reached after many years. She earnestly warned her nuns about the importance of finding a priest who could understand the nature of their souls. She also handpicked the priests for her new Order and made sure they were capable of experiencing the delights that God offered.

We can fear everything, said Teresa, if we let ourselves succumb to the notion of fear. Our imaginations can turn against us and show us scenarios that are very far from the mind of God. Then we worry, which produces nothing but anxiety and doesn't change a thing. And this fear need not be very intense — very often all we experience is a twinge. If we find ourselves worrying over a situation, fear is behind the worrying. And behind that fear is the feeling of not being in control; we do not know what is going to happen, and we are not comfortable with this.

Better that we hand everything over to God, said Teresa, and relax in the knowledge that we are being well cared for.

Meditation

Let yourself gently relax into your place of quiet and peace. Notice any thoughts that may arise — any worries from your daily life, any fears, large or small. Take them all to the divine lap, and place them there. Ask for the divine to take care of them and to help you surrender your control. Ask that your imagination be used for God's communication.

24. Kind Thoughts

The soul could lose its peace and even disturb
the peace of others by going about looking at trifling
things in people that at times are not even imperfections,
but since we know little we see these things
in the worst light. (CW vol. II, 296)

ONE OF HUMANKIND'S GREATEST ENEMIES is judgment. How quick we are to notice the splinter in our sister's or brother's eye without seeing the plank in our own. Teresa, up until the end of her life, was overseeing eighteen monasteries, and the nuns were often housed in very close quarters, where they ate, worked, and prayed together every day. Ample opportunities arose for personalities to conflict and for overzealous religiosity to occur. Teresa quickly became a psychological expert and earned the reputation of having incredible insight into the true nature of any disturbance.

She came to understand judgment as insidious and as the cause of much unrest and lack of love in her nuns. She witnessed that the good intention of helping another could simply be a disguised form of judgment. Very often the advice forthcoming was not solicited, and therefore not welcome, causing offense or a rift in the friendship. The advice could also be irrelevant or not quite accurate, since the situation was being judged according to another's understanding. Teresa wrote, "Ah, if I should have to speak of the mistakes I have seen happen by trusting in the good intention!" (*CW* vol. I, 127). By busying ourselves with another's life, she said, we forget to look at our own life, which is where our attention should be put.

It is not anyone's responsibility to point out the faults of another. Our responsibility is to love. Unfortunately, too many relationships fall into a pattern of judgment in the guise of helping. In particular, our close relationships with our family and intimate partners are prone to this dynamic and can be a major cause of disharmony, since nothing erodes love more quickly than judgment. What one person may perceive as helping can feel like an accusation to another. We must allow others to be, and simply love them as they are. Love has a greater affect than any advice. As a nun once said to me, "The only time people accept advice is when they ask for it."

What do we do then when we find ourselves judging another? Teresa suggested seeking the good in one another and not focusing on faults, whatever we perceive them to be. We are to bring love, not condemnation, into the heart. If we love another, she said, then others' actions should not annoy us. But if we are becoming disturbed, then we should look within to see if those very same faults reside within us. We should not bring them to our friend's attention (unless, of course, they are a major concern); rather, "let each one look to herself," and let mutual love reign.

By looking to our own life, we can overcome the need to help others. Alternatively, we can find appropriate avenues for this need to be expressed. This may be through our profession, through being a volunteer in our community, or simply through being available when friends or family need help. If we can step outside the place of "good intention" and simply be available to love, people will readily seek our counsel or help when it is required. Removing yourself from judgment, from *your own* and from others', and being open to love is the greatest gift you can give the world.

Meditation

Allow yourself to melt into the arms of the divine. Feel yourself being held and loved. Feel your heart open more to the great love there for you. Know that you are loved exactly as you are. Dwell in that love and let it pervade every part of your being. Now see your family, friends, and partner, and love them in the same way. Let the love flow from your heart to theirs. Bask there as long as you can.

25. The Principle of Honor

[The soul] keeps these miserable little rules of etiquette with-
out understanding what honor consists of. And then we shall
reach the point of thinking that we have done a great deal if
we pardon one of these little things. (CW vol. II, 179–80)

HOW OFTEN WE TAKE OFFENSE or enter into battle with others over our personal or cultural pride being wounded and our principles not being publicly honored. Families become estranged, love partnerships suffer serious rifts, and friendships dissolve. For what, Teresa asked? For this matter that we call honor, which is nothing more than a set of rules designed to keep our self-esteem afloat in the public eye. There really is no offense, no injury, no anything at all, said Teresa — only somebody acting in accordance with his or her set of rules, which invariably are not in accordance with our own.

Many times it is only the knowledge of death

(either our own or the other person's) that loosens our grip on our smaller reality, as we are submerged into something much larger than ourselves. We are given new sight from the divine viewing place, and suddenly we see how the rift has no relevance at all to the ultimate connection of love between us.

But death can sometimes be a long time in calling — so what do we do in the meantime? Teresa believed that we can fall into the trap of deciding to forgive the person in question, but with a dose of self-righteousness. We make a personal note that we are the better person for relenting and coming to make peace. Our relationship with the other is not reentered with love and compassion, but with a feeling of superiority. We may publicly be presenting the dove, but privately we are honoring ourselves with the royal crown. However, said Teresa, realistically there is nothing to be forgiven, for all that has been wounded is our mortal pride, not our immortal self. If we can understand how differing realities have collided, and that the only victim is the ego, we could more readily laugh at the sensitivity in which we are so invested.

Very often we hear "it is a matter of principle," and then we usually witness someone stubbornly refusing to move from his or her authorized position. Authorized by whom? Until we choose to ask this question and honestly seek the answer, it is guaranteed that we will continue to take offense and accuse others of causing us personal injury. Honor is something that has been handed down to us from our forebears, and each culture has its own interpretation of it. When we lift away these cultural veils, we will find the very core of our being (and of all beings) in resplendent oneness, free from individual and national identities.

Teresa lived in a time when honor was paramount in society's eyes, and she herself felt deeply bound by it. But then she came to understand that true honor was that which glorified God, and not her. She no longer desired to be honored publicly, nor did her self-esteem require it, as she came to know who the real authority within her soul was. Teresa created the new Carmelite Order, dismissing the normal attentiveness to societal status and honor, and took in converts to Catholicism and those without dowries, which previously did not occur. But most of all, she tirelessly educated her nuns in the importance of laying aside their petty grievances with one another, thereby enabling true love to abide in their monasteries.

Meditation

Let yourself rest gently in the divine arms. Allow any griev-
ances that may be hindering one of your relationships to arise.
See that person before you — open your heart to her or him,
and let love flow between you. Let the smaller ego-self rest in
that love. Bless yourself and the other, and know that you are
both of the one love.

26. Willing Your Way

Whoever tries to grasp too much loses everything; this it seems to me is what will happen here... doing our own will is usually what harms us. (CW vol. II, 158, 314)

AS WE WALK WITH GOD, it is easy to return to running ahead with our own will. Our ever-agile mind can place before us all sorts of plans, and it can even convince us that these plans are God's will. We have been beholden to the whim of our own will and ego for so long that it can, for most us, be a lifelong process to constantly return to the divine desire. For some, like St. Paul, a lightning bolt strikes, or for others, a permanent flash of enlightenment occurs. But for most, it is a long transitional phase of returning to the spirit.

Just the very mention of the word *will* can immediately raise a feeling of protective defiance within us. It is our will, after all, that enables us to engage in our daily living, or so we believe. But we also witness our will guiding us into situations that either do not evolve as we would like or simply crumble despite all our efforts. We can then experience either anger or a sense of deflation and helplessness, as we simply do not get what we want. When this occurs frequently, life can seem too hard, and we either fall into depression or we rally our will even more and push with all our might to make things happen as we desire.

Life was not meant to be so difficult, and as we embrace a more spiritual way of being, this is one of the greatest lessons and gifts that we are given. In receiving this gift, we need to detach from the old way of doing with our smaller (or egoistic) will and to move into the newness of being with our larger (or divine) will. We need to realize that the small will is not being annihilated — it is simply being brought into alignment with the larger will. We still employ it in our daily lives, only now it is in service to a greater love and desire.

God desires for us to experience the purity of love that we are; this is His will, Teresa said. We can travel along many routes in rediscovering this purity, and not all will be of our choosing. If we can remind ourselves of this ultimate divine desire, however, we can more easily lay down our will and surrender it to love. If we become forgetful, as many of us are apt to, Teresa said, then little by little our connection with God becomes obscured. We will find the mind traveling in all directions with all sorts of wondrous plans for us; we will find our desire to spend time with God lessening; and our self-absorption will dramatically increase, and correspondingly our love for others will decrease. Slowly we slip back into the desires of our will, but do not fret, she said, for even though we make ourselves deaf to God's calling, He never ceases to speak our name. Even when we erroneously think we are doing His will, He will send His light to gently bring us back.

But how do we know when it is the divine will? Teresa said that we should constantly ask for it to be so, saying, "Thy will be done," and to take note of our soul. If we find that we are inclined to love more and to have compassion for our fellow beings, and if we do not raise ourselves above others, then we are coming closer to divine love and will.

Meditation

Come into your place of quiet. Invite your small will to enter — allow it to speak any frustrations, anger, or desires. Give these feelings love. Now invite your larger divine will to enter — let it love your smaller will. Let the two merge together in a loving embrace. Allow yourself to be.

27. Your Own Pathway

*It is important to understand that God doesn't
lead all by one path. (CW vol. II, 99)*

WE CAN FEEL VERY VULNERABLE when we begin to
develop our spiritual longings. Like impressionable
children, we are sometimes overly susceptible to the
thoughts and beliefs of others, and there will certainly
be many who readily offer their opinions and advice.
This advice, unfortunately, very often comes from the
giver's frame of reference, that is, from his internal
pathway of being. Though it may be completely successful for him, spiritually and emotionally, it may not
have any relevance to what you need. You are unique,
and so is your pathway to God.

"There are many roads to enter the Heavenly
Father's Kingdom" (John 14:2). Teresa reminds us of

John's words and encourages all of us to live by them, no matter what we see in others or what we feel we need to tell them. It could be that through our very interference we are delaying a valuable lesson that they need to encounter. And what we are essentially saying is, "Come walk on my path, I will show you the way."

We all have the responsibility of developing our own pathway, yet we should be aware of running here or there, constantly seeking advice about which way we should walk. This can become an addictive behavior as we consult divining tools, friends, and even our guiding angels. If we are excessively using these means it is a strong indication that we are not connecting to our own source, our inner God; instead we are looking for a mediator to relay divine messages. This is the old priesthood framework still operating. Yet the way of the mystic is direct communication, and it is available to us all.

Teresa taught that all souls are able to directly enter into relationship with God and did not think her experiences exceptional; she tells of other nuns also receiving the mystical graces. We are all graced with God's love, she said, in whatever way He chooses to express it — we can only make ourselves available to receive it. And then it is our responsibility to take it and live in accordance with whatever is required, be it as a gardener tending to the flowers or as a teacher tending to the people.

Take your feelings of vulnerability with you as you stand before God. Let them become a part of your treasured pathway, and let them show you the way home to your most intimate and fragile self. God adores all of you. There is no expectation about how you should be dressed in your outer garments when you make the divine visit; God sees straight through to your nakedness anyway. Let this vulnerability become a strength, not a weakness, as you show yourself honestly.

Although we are not expected always to know what path to travel on, it is through our internal being and not through external methods designed for others that we will find our way.

Meditation

Feel yourself melting into the divine presence. Allow yourself to come forward in your absolute nakedness — just as you are. Express any feelings of being lost or confused about the pathway you are following — allow God to guide you — and allow yourself to be led.

28. Humoring the Heart

*God deliver me from people so spiritual that they want to
turn everything into perfect contemplation, no matter what.
(CW vol. III, 361)*

THE WORD *SPIRITUALITY* is not synonymous with seriousness. Too often as we embark on our spiritual journey, we fall into the erroneous idea that we are entering
into something very grave indeed. Our sheer eagerness
can become an obstacle to experiencing the playfulness
of the spirit and the lightness of life. Our laughter is a
joy to God and to others — and to our own soul. It is
essential for the health of our being.

Teresa displayed a great sense of humor as she dealt
with her everyday duties, and she was renowned in
social circles for her quick-wittedness in conversation.
Texts also reveal an agile ability for satirical commentary,
in particular regarding matters profoundly "spiritual."

Though deeply respectful of the spiritual treatises, she was able to go beyond their seriousness in favor of a lighthearted satire designed for the pleasure of her religious colleagues. She was no prude, either, as she describes in a letter how, while she was traveling, a lizard got in between her tunic and her bare arm, and she says, "It was through the mercy of God that it didn't get in somewhere else, for I think I would have died, judging from what I felt" (*Letters* no. 108:9, 280). She continues to say that her brother got hold of the lizard, but when he threw it, he hit their traveling companion right in the mouth. This was a great comedy for Teresa, who believed that such traveling experiences lighten the often long and arduous journeys. A good reminder for us as we embark on our own spiritual and physical journeys!

But most of all, Teresa was an expert at laughing at herself and at the workings of her psyche. She found it difficult to take herself too seriously, as she witnessed her smaller ego-self sulk and complain and protectively nurse its wounds over perceived affronts or judgments. How seriously we take our lives and our challenges, she said, and yet how consoled we would be if we were able to laugh at our so-called grievances. In being able to laugh at ourselves, we are able to admit that a greater reality is at play — that the world is not as small as our own ego.

Sensitivity can sometimes be used as a way for more spiritually delicate or artistic souls to remove themselves from the flow of life. However, where does the sensitivity reside? Many believe it to be the very nature of their soul, and they are correct, for the soul is a deeply sensitive being. But when we move into the nature of the *spirit,* the sensitivity of the soul that demands total fidelity to its feelings is no longer relevant. The spirit does not demand or need anything from the outside; the spirit is at peace in whatever environment it is placed.

For many years, we can shun person after person, claiming that they are simply not sensitive enough to us. The reality, however, is that we are not sensitive enough to our *own* being. We have been protecting the delicate ego, and not our true self, as we have so erroneously thought. But we can even laugh about this, because God knows we are not alone! We can take this illusion and let it merge into a new playground of existence, once more bringing the lightness of being into a life lived in, through, and for the spirit.

Meditation

Coming into a place of peace within yourself, allow all the thoughts of the ego to arise. See them from a broader perspective — see how comical many of them are as they jostle for your attention. See how you may take yourself too seriously in your relationships, in your job, in your whole way of being. Allow a lightness to infuse your being, and let the joy of laughter ripple through your spirit and into your soul.

Fourth Dwelling

INTERIOR RECOLLECTION

These are impulses so delicate and refined,
for they proceed from very deep within the interior
part of the soul. (CW vol. II, 367)

I n this dwelling, we are taken into the mystery of the interior workings of the soul. It is here that God teaches us how to listen with the whole of our being. Rather than relying on our own efforts, we let God make the effort for us, taking us deeper into the realm of the spirit.

We are taught age-old meditation practices, accompanied by Teresa's own experiences in dealing with an overactive mind. The value of the intellect and of the body are also offered, implementing a holistic framework for our being. For Teresa, this dwelling characterized the beginning of the true spiritual or supernatural experiences in her life.

29. The Restless Mind

There are some souls and minds so scattered they are like wild horses no one can stop. Now they're running here, now there, always restless. . . . This restlessness is either caused by the soul's nature or permitted by God. (CW vol. II, 107)

TERESA WAS KNOWN for her exceptional intellect and astuteness and was the first woman to be granted the prestigious title of Doctor of the Church. But she struggled with the restlessness and turmoil of her mind: "The noises in my head are so loud that I am beginning to wonder what is going on in it" (*IC,* 77). She found it to be a great interference, both with her writing and her prayer life, but she came to have a unique perspective on a phenomenon that has been the study of many religious traditions.

Teresa likened the mind to the movement of the heavenly bodies of stars and planets and warned against doing ourselves harm by trying to harness this continually moving energy. We should rather bring ourselves into the presence of God. In this way we enter into a gentle and peaceful process, allowing God to take care of the mind instead of forcing our own methods onto it.

She noted that the very effort used in trying not to think of anything, both in our daily living and in meditation, can sometimes rouse the mind to think even more, the concept being that what we resist persists. And there is also the danger that such self-scrutiny will give us a sense of self-importance and self-absorption rather than self-forgetfulness. Another possibility, she believed, is that God may wish to use the mind and intellect to further the divine cause on earth. Who are we to stop this process? As she wrote, "When [God] desires the intellect to stop, He occupies it in another way and gives it a light so far above what we can attain that it remains absorbed. Then without knowing how, the intellect is much better instructed than it was through all the soul's efforts not to make use of it" (*CW* vol. II, 330).

Particularly enlightening is Teresa's belief in the soul's ability to be united with God in the "mansions very near His presence" (*IC,* 77) while our thought runs on in its customary fashion, or in "the outskirts of the Castle." Thus, it is possible for us to connect with the divine self, even while our human self is dealing with the grocery list. Teresa was adamant that those who experienced restlessness, or "monkey mind," while meditating should not cease their practice but should instead connect with the divine presence while thoughts run on. Most of the interior trials and discouragement suffered through the unrest of the mind, she said, can be attributed to a misunderstanding of the workings of our mind and soul.

Ultimately, Teresa is telling us to trust in the workings of God, knowing that what needs to be revealed will be so, regardless of what we may or may not think. By bringing our awareness to the source within rather than focusing on the thoughts without, we allow for a shift in our consciousness that allows for greater communication and for a deeper relationship to develop with our divine self.

Meditation

Let yourself fall gently into the divine tender presence. Allow a feeling of great gentleness to surround you. Let this gentleness permeate every part of your body, mind, and soul. Release any judgment of what you think should or should not be happening, and simply bask in the presence of love. Let your thoughts have the freedom to be, and trust that God will lead you wherever you need to go.

30. The Divine Word

*For one word of His will contains within itself
a thousand mysteries, and thus our understanding
is only very elementary. (CW vol. II, 217)*

OUR SOCIETY IS ONE BASED on many words. Too often these words are used without thought or care to their real meaning, and many of us tend to be verbose in describing the details of our lives. And what occurs when we have to listen to such verbiage? Usually, through sheer self-protection, we alternate between hearing and not hearing. Consequently, we become inattentive to the conversation, with no real communication occurring. Our education and reading have also been centered on a great deal of information and words, in particular on external sources and teaching.

An age-old Christian meditation practice is that called *Lectio Divina* (the Divine Word). In this practice you sit quietly with the scriptures or a work relating to the spirit and ask for guidance in your meditation. Upon opening the book you allow your gaze to fall gently on the page until a particular word or phrase catches your attention. Closing your eyes you softly repeat this word or phrase over and over, allowing it to become part of your breath and to penetrate deep within your body. You allow yourself to be taken into a deep meditative state, and from this place the word of God becomes revealed to you. Your whole body and soul are given a new understanding of this one word or phrase that you have been guided to. Through this transmission your life becomes altered in some way. If you take the same word or phrase tomorrow, and the day after that, and enter into this practice, you may be given another understanding, and another, each affecting your life in a different way. This is what Teresa meant when she said that one word of God contains a thousand mysteries.

Teresa practiced this method of meditation using the Lord's Prayer. She would quietly sit with eyes closed and slowly begin reciting the prayer, allowing the words to guide her. Whenever a particular word or phrase drew her deeper within, she would follow. For instance, repeating "daily bread" over and over, she would allow herself to become absorbed by these words and let God reveal to her one of their many mysteries. In this way she came to know that divine love was her daily manna and sustenance, and that without it she would be unable to live. The connection she was making and living every day with God *was* her daily bread. As she moved into this larger reality, the worries of her smaller life and concerns about literal loaves of bread would dissolve.

The words written through divine inspiration are there for our benefit. Let us take advantage of yet another way in which God seeks to communicate with us. Let us move from the barrage of copious external information to a few words of divine wisdom, allowing our internal source to guide us into the greater mysteries of God. And in our communications with one another, may we pay attention to our words, so that our speech is not an assault on someone's ears and being but rather filled with meaningful expressions of the self.

Meditation

Take time to sit quietly alone with a book of inspiration or spiritual teaching. Ask that you be guided to the word or phrase most needed for you right now. Alternatively, you may simply ask that a word or phrase be given to you. Begin softly repeating it over and over, allowing it to fill your whole body and mind. Allow its wisdom to come forth, and accept it with every cell of your body. Give thanks.

31. Discursive Reflection

It involves a gradual increase of self-control
and an end to a vain wandering from the right path;
it means conquering, which is making use of one's senses
for the sake of the inner life. (CW vol. II, 148)

OUR MINDS ARE FILLED with personal aspirations, secret desires, our children's school plays, the checkout clerk's smile, and dental appointments to be kept — and this is just on Monday! The whirlwind of our external life is continually occurring in our minds as we strive to keep up with all our responsibilities. But having committed to our internal life we must find methods to facilitate our continued exploration. Some days it is easier than others to be present to our inner realm, which Teresa knew only too well.

When she was having trouble reaching a state of calm, she would reflect on the life of Christ. In this way her intellect and imagination would be engaged and would cease to run here and there with wild imaginings and storytelling. She also discovered how beneficial this type of meditation could be for the soul, opening her awareness to realms she never thought possible and revealing "deep secrets" of Christ's life. In this way a love affair with both the *human* and the *divine* Christ began for her. How can we love someone we do not know? she asked. And so she would spend time in this way, following the human Christ on his journey and learning of his divine nature as he encountered, and gave to, the world. This enabled her to recognize her own Christ-like journey as she was shown parallels to the life she was asked to live.

Teresa would often visit Christ in the Garden of Gethsemane and hear the midnight prayer of his knowing — of the upcoming betrayal and abandonment he was about to face. She held his hand in the depths of the night, just as He held hers in the times of her darkness. She would follow Him to the cross and wipe His brow and give Him water, forgiving His tormentors for their ignorance. Subsequently, she forgave her own tormentors. She would also take great delight in seeing the Christ child make clay birds that would transmute and fly, and her own innocence would return upon her recognition that miracles can be created by all, with the grace of God. These meditations helped reveal her own human and divine nature working as one and gave her courage in times of loneliness or difficulty. They brought her closer to the One who was ever-present within her.

Christ's energy is resolute and loving, that is, firmly grounded in the truth of being. By meditating on this energy, whether in the personal form of the earthly Christ or in the more abstract energetic form, we can enter our own heavenly inner realm and bring it forth into the world through our words and actions.

Meditation

Bringing yourself into a place of stillness, let an episode of Christ's life appear to you. Observe and absorb the realness of His humanity — allow yourself to feel His feelings.

Feel the very essence of His nature and see how this determines who He is and how He responds to the situation. Feel your own humanity. Feel your own essence. See how you can take all these into the world.

32. Use of the Intellect

Lack of knowledge causes the afflictions of many people . . . interior trials . . . melancholy and loss of health.
(CW vol. II, 320)

AS WE REBOUND from the Age of Reason and come to acknowledge the other faculties that we have been blessed with, let us not swing too far on the pendulum and disregard how the intellect can be used for our benefit. A common phrase we hear today is "it is only the mind," and subsequently we throw all thoughts away. But sometimes those thoughts could be telling us something that we need to know. This tendency to suspend our intellectual faculties when we engage in our spiritual life can have unfortunate and unnecessary consequences. Everything can be used in returning home. It is a matter of knowing how and when, of knowing which faculties are most beneficial — it is a matter of discernment.

Teresa made the distinction between the mind and the intellect. She understood the mind to be the smaller self, with its constant requests, questions, and worries. The intellect, on the other hand, is a sophisticated tool that we can use in returning to God. Along with writing about her interior life, she also enjoyed speaking with knowledgeable people who understood the states of being she was describing. To give form to her experiences, through words, enabled her to have a deeper understanding and confirmation of her own life.

Articulating her interiority was something Teresa sometimes struggled with, but she realized the great value of doing so. It not only served as a guide to others having similar experiences, but it also acted as a reminder for her when she encountered doubt or confusion. The intellect can be especially helpful in these times, she said, since it can remind us of past times when we erroneously succumbed to these doubting states. It can speak to us of what we *know* to be true and can aid us in not becoming flooded by emotions and thoughts that can take us further away from God. Likewise, when we may feel old insecurities arise, the intellect can remind us that these feelings are no longer necessary, that we do not need to revisit the past in order to live confidently in the present. The intellect can tell us, again and again, that wonderful story of how we are loved.

What we have learned from past mistakes is always recorded by the intellect and can be accessed at any time. We can ask that the intellect be used for our higher good, and we can use it for our own and the world's advancement. The intellect, when openly connected with the divine presence, can also be used to bring forward all types of wonderful inventions, whether technological, environmental, or in the realm of human development. If used in service to God and to humanity, then it can only be for the good of all.

The intellect is the container of knowledge — not what we have been told, but what we have experienced — and also more. It enables us to enter the divine realm of knowledge, of *gnosis*. It can take us places and show us things that the divine intellect is creating and thinking and making available to us. Let us honor the intellect's role in our life, for in denying any part of ourselves, we are denying God.

Meditation

Letting the mind come into a place of rest, call forth your intellect. Ask that it be divinely inspired, and offer it to serve the greater good of all. Allow your natural gift of discernment to come before you, and give thanks for its wisdom. Open yourself to receiving that wisdom. Honor your past mistakes and let yourself learn from them. Let your intellect be guided by God in bringing whatever you need right now.

33. In the Body

To be always withdrawn from corporeal things . . . is the trait
of angelic spirits not of those who live in mortal bodies.
(CW vol. II, 399)

AS WE DRAW DEEPER into our interior being, our soul
can become a welcome place of refuge from the world
and all its craziness. Life as we know it can then start to
look a little unappealing, wearying the soul and body.
We may feel sorely tempted to opt out of this vital
cycle. We may claim that it is too hard to deal with all
the emotional stirrings not only of our own soul but
also of those around us. We can use our inner castle of
peace to escape from life rather than to fully enter it.

Many people, if not all, have at some time in their
lives experienced a traumatic event. A trauma is any
experience in which the body and soul have gone into

shock, both physical and psychological. Depending on the soul involved, psychological shock may come from being verbally attacked. For others, something more severe may have to occur before shock sets in. There is no set formula for what brings about shock, but we do know that everyone who suffers from it experiences a flight of the soul from the body. The soul is fleeing to safety.

Spirituality can, in some instances, become a safe haven. In developing our contact with other realms and beings we sometimes escape to these places when life becomes too difficult. We can withdraw into our own spiritual world and then erroneously convince ourselves that what we are experiencing is the *true* spirituality. In this way we divorce ourselves, at least in part, from the world. Teresa warned of the danger of such belief and was adamant that we were given these bodies to live in and not to escape from. She said that we must not flee from the things of this world, that we must look to the lives of those who have, in mortal bodies, accomplished great things for God. Take these people as your companions, she said, and know that forsaking your humanity is not the pathway to God.

If the soul is not fully present in the body, then we cannot be fully present to life.

We have a responsibility to ourselves and to those we share the planet with to be as fully present as possible; otherwise, life passes us by, or perhaps more accurately, we pass life by. Often when we are confronted with a situation that we would rather not be involved in, we tend to withdraw, if not physically, then energetically. By doing this we distance ourselves from our source of being, diminishing the strength of who we are and what we can give to the world.

Teresa, in all her wisdom, understood this completely and was known for her frankness and complete honesty, both with herself and with others. In this way she awakened not only herself but also the many who lived and worked with her and sought her counsel. Likewise, we are all here to help awaken one another through the honesty of our being.

Meditation

Coming into your place of quiet, breathe deeply into the core of your body. Feel the soul and the body as one, and notice the strength you feel through this union. Allow any circumstances in which you feel a disconnection from one or the other to arise. Let your inner guiding presence join whatever separation has occurred. Bring this essence of union into your life.

34. Care of the Body

*The changes in the weather and the rotating
of the bodily humors often have the result that . . . souls
cannot do what they desire. . . . If they seek to force
themselves more during these times, the bad condition
becomes worse and lasts longer. (CW vol. I, 118)*

IN A WORLD OBSESSED with productivity there is very little understanding of the need for genuine rest. People collapse at the end of the workweek, which for many is six days long, and the rest they do receive is more a "topping off" of energy rather than a revitalization. We have been programmed to produce at all times, at all costs, even if it means compromising our health. We skip meals and tell ourselves that energy bars will suffice, forgetting the importance of the slow, natural process of digestion and the enjoyment of our food. Illness lurks in our overly tired systems and very often strikes at what we consider the most inconvenient times — when our deadlines need to be met!

What is also common today is the need for a long-overdue emotional assessment of our soul. Sometimes when we fail to do this, our soul can override bodily functions and stop us in our tracks. It demands that we take notice of our internal workings that have been so conveniently ignored and placed aside as we busily attend to our lives. We need to become attentive to our bodies and our health, to listen to them daily so that we do not become overloaded — for as the soul can affect the body, so can the body affect the soul.

What is required, said Teresa, again is the gift of discernment. We must come to know what is occurring in our body so that we can ably treat our ailments. When the body needs to rest we should not resist but take time out from our duties and responsibilities. Even if the voice of recrimination reminds us that we should be "doing something," we are to ignore it and go bask in the sun. Likewise, if our body is ailing and needs particular foods, then feed it what it requires. Teresa often recommended variations in diet when the nuns were not well. She was not fanatical about restrictions, even during Lent. Common sense goes a long way, she said, and as the body goes through changes, so must we adapt accordingly.

However, we must also be aware of the stirrings of the soul, she said, since sometimes the body's ills are bringing us a deeper message. We should be aware of the real need; otherwise, we will be living in constant pain and illusion. Discernment, Teresa said, is the key and is born through love — love for oneself and for the truth of one's being. When this is practiced, one's life will move forward, with changes continually occurring and "the bodily humors rotating."

Teresa experienced a great deal of illness, which in the latter years came about principally through her not heeding her own advice. She would work right through the night answering correspondence and dealing with business matters, sleeping only a few hours. Her physician advised her that without adequate rest she would continue to be plagued by her illnesses. Even though she relieved other nuns of their duties in times of necessity, she did not give herself the same opportunity. Sometimes we are harsher with ourselves than we need to be — even if we do make sainthood!

Meditation

Allow yourself to fall into a place of deep rest — sink deeper and deeper into the body. Allow your attention to move slowly through all the parts of the body, internal and external, and openly listen. What is your body telling you? Let it speak its wisdom. Allow yourself to follow its words and advice. Love yourself in all honesty.

35. The Living Water

*To the other fountain the water comes direct
from its source, which is God . . . for the water is flowing
all the time. (IC, 81)*

JESUS TOLD THE SAMARITAN WOMAN, "Whoever drinks
of this water will never thirst" (John 4:14). As we journey deeper into our interior castle our thirst begins to
change. Slowly, we leave the yearnings for the material
world behind as we acknowledge that our throat is
always parched and never satisfied. We turn ever more
faithfully toward the divine source, thirsty for real water.
Our commitment to our soul growth now begins to
flourish, and it may feel as though we are being carried
on a flowing stream with little effort on our part. This
is the eternal spring, said Teresa; this is God satisfying
the real thirst of the soul.

Teresa distinguished between striving to come to

know God and allowing God to come meet us. When we strive, she said, it is like a vessel being filled with water coming from far away; many aqueducts and other ingenious inventions are needed to guide the water and to keep it flowing toward, and into, the vessel. This process, she says, is comparable to using various meditation techniques and intellectual faculties to reach God — it is through our own effort that we bring our human nature to the divine — and as Teresa experienced, it can be quite noisy!

When God comes to meet us, there is no need for aqueducts or any other means of assistance; the vessel is effortlessly being filled by the divine and flowing spring. It need not travel long distances, since the wellspring is right there. This produces the greatest peace and quiet, deep within the soul. There is no effort and no noise, only a feeling of sweetness, incomparable to anything the soul has ever known. And then, said Teresa, this feeling, this *living water,* flows through all the dwelling places of the soul, filling all the faculties, and reaching the body itself. The whole being — mind, body, and soul — overflows with spiritual delight. This is a gift, wrote Teresa, that "has its source in God and ends in ourselves" (*IC,* 81).

As this living water flows through us it cleanses our soul, and we can find ourselves armed with an even more resolute desire to follow the divine will. Fear has no place here, and whereas before we may have secretly feared what God had in store for us, we now understand that only good can arise from drinking this living water. The soul recognizes the real thirst and the real water.

Having no fear, the vessel continually experiences the abundance of the overflowing spring. Those small and large miracles in our lives occur so naturally. If, however, fear sneaks back in, as it is wont to do, back we go to mending the aqueducts. But take heart, said Teresa; our God will revisit when we least expect it — all we can do is prepare the way and know that we are making our way home at the pace that God desires.

Meditation

Bring yourself into the presence of love — know that it is right there for you. Let go of all your spiritual efforts, all your desires, and your will to know God. Simply rest in your being. Allow the waters of love to fill your soul and body. Know that you need never thirst again.

36. Expansion of the Soul

As this heavenly water begins to flow from this source of which I am speaking — that is, from our very depths — it proceeds to spread within us and cause an interior expansion and produce ineffable blessings. (IC, 82)

IN OUR MODERN AGE, with its great emphasis on the discipline of psychology, it can be easy to remain only in the realm of the psyche and to forget the deeper place within us, that is, our spiritual being. Returning to the "heart" and what it feels is an essential component for many of us who have been disengaged from these feelings for so long. However, our spiritual journey now moves us into realms far exceeding where the heart can take us. We are being moved into the depths of feeling with the *whole* of our being and not just into the isolated parts that we have come to know.

Teresa was not afraid to reach deep within her soul and to feel God's movement within her. She followed the living water as it flowed through her being and came to understand the differences between the feelings of the heart and the feelings of the soul. *Cum dilatasti cor meum:* "You have given me freedom of the heart" (Psalm 118:32). Teresa used this biblical reference, which the Carmelites would recite at prayer, to further her thoughts on the subject. She understood this freedom in terms of expansion and felt that when only the heart is engaged, we experience constriction. The heart causes tears to flow, and sometimes it is difficult to stop them, as our emotions also contribute to their ongoing release. That is, she was describing the psychological cleansing of our heart wounds.

The feeling of expansion, on the other hand, she described as coming from a much deeper place than the heart — it is at the very center of the soul. Here, she said, the soul perceives the very fragrance of God, sweet-smelling perfumes that spread through the entire soul. Yet there is no physical scent of perfume, "for the experience is more delicate than an experience of these things" (*CW* vol. II, 325). She said that this sweetness allows the soul to expand until it can understand the many secrets contained within, and a great freedom is felt by the whole being. This is not an emotional experience but one in which the emotions are at rest and the heart is at peace. The feelings that arise here are the deep stirrings of the soul that connect it to the greater mystery of all life. She claimed that the experience of the soul is not superior to that of the heart — they are simply different, and we will be taken into each one depending on what we require for our growth.

It would benefit us, in our psychological age, to take note of this distinction that Teresa made and to be aware of becoming caught in the heart experience only. By believing this to be the extent of our experience and awareness, we limit ourselves to feeling only our emotions, and we don't feel the true depth of our soul. Like Teresa, we need not be afraid of these depths; rather, we can dive into the freedom and expansion they give us. Although fear can arise at such a thought, remember, God has our best interests at heart, and the depths of our soul feelings are our friends, not our enemies. To feel deeply is to find our innate bliss and to live in great awareness and connection with ourselves and with each other.

Meditation

Bring yourself into a place of deep being and stillness. Enter the breath, and gradually lower yourself into the depth of your being. If any fear arises, hand it over to God and let yourself sink even further. Feel what it is like to enter the depth of your soul. Feel any yearnings or desires, and allow your natural state of bliss to overcome you. Revel in this state and know it is yours. Bless yourself and all life around you.

37. The Enigma of Gender

*The one who thinks less and has less desire
to act does more. (CW vol. II, 329)*

*I sat down under the shadow of Him whom I desired
and His fruit was sweet to my taste. (Song of Songs 2:3)*

IN THIS TIME OF SPIRITUAL AWAKENING we are all being
called to reclaim the mystique of *both* the feminine and
the masculine principles. We have been taught that the
feminine encapsulates the state of being and that the masculine encompasses the state of doing. However, this
interpretation comes from society's expectation of the
male and female roles rather than from an understanding of the inherent nature of these energies. In *Mysterium Coniunctionis*, C. G. Jung maintains that the
feminine nature relates to the secrets contained in
the physical world and is the active principle; its goal
is to seek union with all that exists (89). The masculine relates to the spiritual world and is the passive

principle; it has discrimination as its goal. That is, women initiate and bring things *into* being (and prod the men to help as well), while the men are busy dreaming and deciding which way is best (discriminating). The ideal, of course, is the union of both. This unification of the innate female and male principles can be manifested in all men and women, so that all "doing" emerges from a place of "being," in all individuals.

Teresa believed that we can save all our effort by sitting beneath the tree of divine love; it is here that we are given inspirations to act on. And if they are divine in origin, then we can be confident that their fruition is guaranteed. We need not think them out or strive for them — "there's no need to move the hand or raise it" (*CW* vol. II, 249) — for the Beloved has already picked the fruit, cooked it, and even chewed it for us. In this way, "His fruit is sweet to our taste," and there is no effort on our part. All we need to do is allow our souls to come into the sweetness of repose (the masculine). From there, we move forward with our divine inspirations, turning them into actions (the feminine). In this way, and not through our specific desires, which are dubious at the best of times, we can be assured that we are bringing profit to other souls. When we are *not* trying is when we are divinely doing; if we are making an effort, then we are "humanly" doing.

Teresa was highly developed in both the masculine and feminine energies and brought them into a unification that allowed her work to flourish. She knew, though, how quickly the thinking mind could enter and take her down the path of human rational deduction. By following this path, she says, we will experience mental fatigue and delusion. Know that it is a rare occasion for the spirit to be rational!

We women and men of today are being asked to look deep inside ourselves at the true *mystique* of our inner masculine and feminine powers. We are to profoundly feel all that we are and what we embody. We need not be afraid of the historical abuses by the feminine and masculine forms (for there has been damage caused by both); we can find the truth of these beautiful energies within ourselves. We can then bring them forward in unity as the true gift that they, and we, are.

Meditation

Sit beneath the tree of divine love — bask in its shade. Let your male self feel free to sit there as long as it likes, tasting the fruits and listening to the divine inspirations whispering in his ear. When you feel ready, come back to this physical world and let those inspirations take form in your life, allowing your female self to bring them into being. Bless both your masculinity and your femininity, and allow them to merge in a union of love.

38. The Prayer of Quiet

Don't think this recollection is acquired by the intellect striving to think about God within itself, or by the imagination imagining Him within itself... what I am speaking of comes in a different way. (CW vol. II, 328)

As we become accustomed to spending time in stillness with ourselves and with God, we may come to notice a natural quietness beginning to develop in our soul. We may feel it anytime during the day or night, whether we are engaged in activity or in meditation. During these times we are remembering the divine within, with the soul naturally coming to rest in a state of calm. It is not something we actively enter into; rather, we are taken into the arms of He who loves us. We are bidden to lie peacefully there, as if in a dream-like sleep, yet being fully awake at the same time. We are being taught how to be present to God.

Teresa described this recollection as a natural and

gentle drawing inward of the senses; our attention is no longer on the external world but on our interior one. It is through this recollection that we are being prepared to listen. In this way the soul, rather than striving to be in constant discourse, now becomes attentive, with an awareness of the workings of God. All we need to do, said Teresa, is to look at God. There is no need here for intellectual reflections or conceptual thoughts, only the desire to see His face. As we desire, so we are given.

In this quiet prayer Teresa emphasized the need to be totally present with God, to not turn our backs or close our eyes to Him. In not being present we are unable to hear; in closing our eyes we are unable to see. All harm comes, she said, from not understanding that He is near and in imagining Him as far away. She comically noted that if we seek Him in heaven, then it would be necessary to go a long way! She then adds, with more seriousness, that she knows heaven to be within us, since this is where the God of heaven truly resides. Like St. Augustine, who searched for God in every external place and finally found Him within, Teresa constantly draws us back to ourselves again and again.

In coming to know this God of heaven as very close to us, we can come to behold unceasing and magnificent beauty and love, that is, the face of God. For some, such beauty and radiance is difficult to look on; others allow themselves only glimpses before running back into the less dazzling state that they are used to. Whatever the case may be, ask that you be given

God's eyes to see with, and looking through these divine eyes of glory, see Him gazing at you with the tender strength of love.

It is a gift, said Teresa, to come into this prayer of quiet, but the more we are available to the presence of God through drawing ourselves into a place of interior recollection, the more we feel His presence. We then more readily accept this remembrance of divine presence as our true state of being, and it can enter into our lives as a lived reality.

Meditation

Quietly withdrawing from your external environment, come into the interior of your being. Breathe deeply into your internal space — allow the state of calm to infuse your soul. Allow the God within to rise and greet you, and let your soul be absorbed in the great and tender love. Keep yourself attentive to this presence and let yourself see with the eyes of God.

Fifth Dwelling

SURRENDER

*That soul has now delivered itself into His hands
and His great love has so subdued it that it neither knows
nor desires anything save that God shall do
with it what He wills. (IC, 109)*

W e are called to the ever-present and ongoing journey of surrendering ourselves to the divine will. Through this continual act of surrender we come to find our essential nature and thus our true freedom. Even though at times we may find ourselves dying a painful death to our old concept of self, we will discover great treasures in giving ourselves over to God's desire.

In this dwelling we question our motives for following the spiritual pathway. What are our expectations of God? Do we only want our own will fulfilled? These and other questions are placed before us, revealing the true nature of our spiritual journey. Whatever the answers, the open arms of God are waiting to receive us and to guide us back into the truth of our being.

39. Expectations of the Spiritual Life

*For perfection as well as its reward does not consist
in spiritual delights but in greater love and in deeds done
with greater justice and truth. (CW vol. II, 313)*

SOMETIMES WE ARE ASKED to look at our motivations for walking the spiritual path. Do we merely seek peace of mind? Are we only concerned with experiencing blissful moments of divine rapture? Or do we wish to serve for the glorification of the divine? A common trap that many fall into is succumbing to the ego's desire to *obtain* something from spirituality. Using the camouflage of spiritual terminology, the ego cleverly disguises its goal to serve itself, not God. We freely speak our higher truths, but more often than not the ego is simply doing what it does best: controlling everything.

For instance, we may fabricate a peaceful sanctified

existence by only allowing into our sphere people who won't upset our equilibrium — those who don't challenge us or who do not reflect our own negativity. Previously, when confronted with difficult situations or people, both reflections of the ego, we have either projected our own unresolved feelings back onto them, or we have simply run in the other direction (the fight-or-flight syndrome). The ego now tells us in its sophisticated voice that negativity has no spiritual benefit and that we would do well to remove ourselves from this situation or person immediately. We are still in flight; we are moving away from, not toward — as the ego would have us believe — our greater selves.

Using this strategy, the ego protects itself from experiencing any upset to its controlled way of life and externally creates a peaceful landscape that allows it to live temporarily in an illusory state of peace and bliss. I am not saying that peace of mind and bliss are always illusionary, only that we too often mistake the by-product of our spiritual lives for the goal. By making peace and bliss the only goals, we pass by true spirituality, which is service that honors God, not self, which in its turn brings real peace and bliss.

Teresa's acid test for any action, vision, or spiritual revelation was to discern whether it glorified God and whether it consisted of loving our neighbor. She was well aware of the ego's need to glorify itself, and she was vigilant in her awareness of its many tricks and clever debating tactics. She always turned herself toward divine love and asked to be shown the truth of her desires and actions, and as a consequence, she experienced many deaths of her ego. Her goal was to love, and to live that love in the world as it existed. From this love flowed those delicate and precious moments of peace radiating through the whole of her being. This is a deep peace that others cannot disturb or remove, no matter how antagonistic or negative they are.

This same peace may flow into and through us if we make love and service to God our spiritual goals. It takes courage to be honest with ourselves, and often the work is painful, since it demands that the smaller self continuously die to itself and its conceptions. The rewards, however, are far greater than the ego's illusions, as we open the divine door to our true loving and divine self.

Meditation

Take time to sit in stillness and ask yourself honestly about the goal of your spiritual path. What is your true motivation and desire? It does not matter what reply you receive, only that it is given in full honesty. Call on divine assistance to lead you closer to the fullness of your inner love, and ask that you be able to share and live this love in truth with all you meet, regardless of who they may be and what they may bring you.

40. Dying into Love

Sustain me with flowers and surround me with apples,
for I am dying with love. (Song of Songs 2:5)

WITH SO MUCH EMPHASIS PLACED on individuality and preservation of the self in our society, the idea of surrendering to another is an anathema. We have been taught to become self-reliant and independent and have taken these teachings to the extreme; as a result, we have successfully alienated ourselves from one another, in the process also estranging ourselves from God. Even when we are diligently following our spiritual path, it is easy to keep a little of us quietly hidden away, and guaranteed, this hidden self, who still thinks it is separate from God, will be planning and scheming our life path. When we truly surrender, there is no hidden self and no separation, and it is God who does all the planning.

Teresa noted that our reputation becomes a huge obstacle to surrendering. Even when we are working for the benefit of others, we can temper our words or actions so as not to displease the other. We choose not to create an awkward situation, and therefore we retreat from our inner knowing and call it "discretion." Falling into the justification of discretion, said Teresa, is nothing more than sheltering ourselves from the fear of being persecuted, that is, of having our reputation tarnished. She maintained that the souls who do the most good are those who do not care if they displease their fellow men and women. Once a priest asked her if it would be beneficial for him to accept the office of bishop. Her reply was divinely inspired; she told him that only when he did not desire authority should he accept it. That is, only when he no longer cared about his reputation would he be able to fulfill the position credibly.

God does not want us to withhold anything, said Teresa. "He will have it all for Himself" (*IC*, 97). And the more we surrender to God, the more divine inspiration we shall receive. When we take this inspiration into the world, free from worries about our reputation, then other souls will also benefit. Teresa said that she could not think of anything more wonderful than seeing another soul advancing toward the truth of their God. This, she said, is the fruit of the flowers spoken of in the above quote from the Song of Songs; it is souls helping one another to return home.

Teresa metaphorically died of love when she was

able to relinquish her reputation by not caring about what was being said about her. She received numerous criticisms, both behind her back and to her face regarding her divinely guided insights about the reform of the Order. However, she was released from worry when she was shown that these instances were beneficial for all souls concerned. If she had retreated from her guidance, all her work on this earth would have been jeopardized.

In what way do we retreat from our spiritual inspirations and insights? Do we use "discretion" as an excuse for not revealing ourselves fully in order to protect our reputation? In a world where public image is highly valued it is easier to live in the mainstream of existence, validating our separation from our spirituality as a means of survival. Ironically, when we release the separation we will no longer be surviving, we will be flourishing.

Meditation

Fall into the gentleness of your loving self. Release any anxiousness or worry. Allow your hidden self to come forward — let it voice its concerns — and then gently lay it down in God's loving arms. Feel the two become one. Dwell in this unity. Ask to be guided in your life according to divine love. Surrender.

41. The Hidden Treasure

Soul, you must seek yourself in Me
And in yourself seek Me. (CW vol. III, 385)

THE FOUNDING FATHERS of the Carmelite Order were hermits who gathered on Mount Carmel in the Holy Land during the early days of Christendom, and they lived a solitary life of prayer and contemplation. Their aim was to seek and find God, the pearl of the hidden treasure. Teresa reminds us of the fathers' original quest, saying that we must return to these simple origins and not become distracted by other desires and by more complex philosophical pathways. We must strengthen the soul and dig for this treasure, she said, to discover the truth about where this pearl resides.

As we progress further into the castle, we must remain sincere about and faithful to our journey. Too easily we become distracted: we may simply become a little lazy about our meditation and prayer time; we may feel it is more important to be working for the good of others in the world; or others may influence our priorities. Before we realize what has occurred we may find ourselves disconnected from our source and less balanced in ourselves. Return to your inner dwelling, said Teresa. In a writing in which she converses with her God, He says through her,

> *Soul, since you are My room,*
> *My house and dwelling,*
> *If at any time,*
> *Through your distracted ways*
> *I find the door tightly closed,*
> *Outside yourself seek Me not. (CW vol. III, 385)*

If you really wish to find God, said Teresa, do not go here and there but seek the one you wish to find in yourself. And you do not need to shout or constantly repeat your desire, for God is not deaf. Nor do we need to turn our eyes upward to heaven, for the Beloved is right here waiting for us.

Just as God is within us, so are we within God. In the same writing Teresa gave us this beautiful description (God is speaking):

> *With such skill, soul,*
> *Love could portray you in Me*
> *That a painter well gifted*

Could never show
So finely that image. (CW vol. III, 385)

The image of us within God, merging with the ineffable being of love, defies all description. The thought of this union and the very possibility of such expansiveness humble us in awe, and yet this is who we are. And this expansiveness equally dwells within:

For love you were fashioned
Deep within me. (CW vol. III, 385)

A symbiotic relationship is occurring, continuously moving in and through the human equation of being, whether or not we are aware of it.

Fortunate are those who are given a taste of *knowing* this unity. This knowing, said Teresa, does not come about through seeing a vision or hearing a message or even through understanding, but rather, it is a certainty *felt* within the soul. This certainty, she says, can only be placed there by God and never leaves the soul, even if it never experiences it again. And we must not bother to look for reasons why this certitude comes about — this unity is not for understanding — all we need do is simply accept the divine gift graciously.

Meditation

Place all desires, distractions, and thoughts aside and come into your own stillness. Open yourself to receive the hidden treasure that lies within — know that this has always been with you and always will be, that this is who you are. Feel this treasure merge with the greater love that surrounds you. This is also you. Marvel at who you are.

42. Drinking the Wine

The King brought me into the wine cellar
and set charity in order within me. (Song of Songs 2:4)

AT TIMES WE CAN BECOME OVERWHELMED by the maintenance that our spiritual life requires, and we may also feel like we are not making any progress. It is essential that we do not pay heed to these thoughts but rather that we give of ourselves with even greater abandon into the arms of God. If we cannot do this, we risk becoming like the bride in the Song of Songs (3:2), who searches in every part of the city for her Beloved but does not find Him anywhere. It is better, said Teresa, that we let God make the effort. How quickly we forget that it is God who is setting the love within us and that we do not, at this stage, even need to let Him in.

The King *brings* the bride into the wine cellar; she does not come of her own accord. In fact, said Teresa, the King also *places* her there, without the need for opening doors or even for entering, just as the resurrected Christ appeared in the disciples' room without their opening the door (John 20:19). It is the same when our soul enters the Holy of Holies. We enter the very center of our soul without entering; we are brought there in the same way that the bride is brought to the wine cellar: by love itself.

The wine cellar is filled with the most delectable wines, and, wrote Teresa, God wishes for us to drink from all of them and to become completely inebriated. God wants to keep nothing from us, and as we grow accustomed to drinking from this cellar we find that we are "going out of our selves" (*CW* vol. II, 251); that is, we are given the ability to love others in ways that we have not experienced before. This is the sacred gift given, through the inebriation of the soul, as it leaves its old ways behind and embraces divine loving. This is what is meant by "and set charity in order within me." The magic of love is alive, and we provide the vehicle for it to be manifested on this earth.

Let us not be fearful when we feel ourselves being transformed by this divine wine, said Teresa, since our weaker nature (the ego) is blessed to die such a death. And if we feel the need to understand how the inebriated soul can be of service to God, we can turn to Mary the Mother. When visited by the Archangel Gabriel, who was relaying the message of her upcoming pregnancy, she asked, "How can this be?" But after he answered, "The Holy Spirit will come upon you; the power of the Most High will overshadow you," she had no further questions and simply said yes to what was being given to her (Luke 1:34–35). Her understanding went beyond the power of human reasoning; her soul *and her body* were gifted with the wisdom of a divine love that allowed her to believe in the seeming folly of God. I am sure that through carrying the infant Jesus, her whole being became further inebriated and changed.

It can be frightening when we feel internal changes occurring, and at times they can occur quite rapidly. We can literally feel like we are "outside ourselves" or that we are somebody else, and this is quite true. We are, for this moment, out of our old ego-self and emerging into the light of the world, having given one of the *many* births to our higher self. May we take delight in this death and subsequent rebirth, and as Teresa wrote, "Let it die in this paradise of delights" (*CW* vol. II, 252).

Meditation

Feel your stillness and your natural state of being. Allow yourself to be brought into the very wine cellar of love. Let yourself drink randomly, without reason or plan, from the divine wine of love. Say yes to whatever you are given. Place any fear to the side, and keep drinking of the love. Let an old self die — let a new self be born. Say yes to this paradise of delights.

43. Union of Wills

And that He may show His marvels more clearly
He doesn't want our will to have any part to play.
(CW *vol. II, 340*)

A MINISTER ONCE SAID TO ME, "The only time my
will and the divine will are going to join is when I
die." And so it may feel to many of us. But Teresa
believed that it is possible for our wills to be united
with God's desire for us. And this unification need not,
and probably will not, occur in one almighty leap of
surrender. Far more realistic and common is a slow
relinquishment of our will to the divine command.

Traveling in the fifth dwelling, said Teresa, it is clear
that *in some way* our wills are united with God's. Although they are not entirely surrendered, still there are
moments of unity that bring the soul into the dominion
of universal love. This unification can take on varied

forms according to God's desires. Being united with God's will, she believed, does not automatically eradicate experiences that cause us pain, though the intensity and the length of their duration can lessen considerably. There are also many different kinds of suffering. Sometimes we are moved by compassion for another's pain, and we empathically feel their distress — our love for them gives us entry into their feelings. Likewise, we may feel a similar painful compassion for the whole of humanity as we witness the ever-evolving cycle of power and conflict spreading throughout the world. Jesus and the Buddha were both known for such compassion. Jesus showed this as he healed the sick, and his deep feelings were displayed as he encountered the death of Lazarus (John 11:33–36). The Buddha's compassion and depth of feeling led him to seek an end to the universal suffering that he witnessed. His teachings on the true nature of reality have helped many and continue to do so today.

There are also, however, the sufferings that occur on our spiritual pathway that may be difficult to endure. Teresa wrote, "In one way or another, there must be a cross while we live" (*CW* vol. II, 345). However, if we embrace the cross, that is, accept it as part of our journey, then it is easier to bear. If we drag it along unwillingly, then it hurts and wearies us, and it feels as though the pain will never cease. Jesus, in his divinity, knew the sufferings that lay before him. And in his humanity, he asked that he be spared them. In surrendering his will completely, he said, "Not my will, but yours be done."

In learning to surrender our will, we must not judge ourselves when we feel ourselves resisting or denying the divine imperative. We will be given plenty more opportunities to join in the divine partnership. In doing so we will experience the liberation of the soul, even if at the time it may not be readily apparent. Teresa knew that the tranquillity of the soul ultimately rested in this union of wills and encouraged all to take refuge there, where nothing — not sickness, poverty, or death — could affect our inner peace.

Meditation

Place yourself in the divine light and let yourself rest lightly and peacefully. Put all desires, even spiritual ones, to the side. Simply bask in the light, and let the divine will love you and guide you as it desires. Allow your trust to grow.

44. It Is Not about Me

I live without living in myself...
I die because I do not die. (CW vol. III, 375)

WITH ALL THE CURRENT EMPHASIS on psychological healing and inner journeying, an ethos of self-absorption can be created. We may become so focused on our inner life and its workings that we remove ourselves from the greater matrix of life. Not only does this deprive us of much-needed support, but it also leads to our losing our place in the world. As a result, we may feel a sense of loss and disconnection, and our emotions may overwhelm and even engulf us. We can be fooled into thinking that this is part of the process that we need to endure; however, when we do not understand our lives in greater context, we can lose our anchor and subsequently ourselves.

Teresa was extremely vigilant with her nuns and was quick to recognize the validity of true "spiritual tears," that is, those given by God, which produced a feeling of sweetness in the soul. The other kinds of tears, which focused on the misery of the self, were produced from an internal imbalance. Her advice for dealing with the latter was to restrict, or in some cases, to remove those persons from private prayer time and to engage them in activities designed to help the community. In this way their attention was no longer wholly focused on themselves but was brought back into the communal context. She noted that some temperaments were simply not suited for long periods of inner reflection, and she was rigorous in her selection process of prospective nuns.

She also looked to the example of Christ. How is it, she asked him in prayer, that he did not collapse into himself through the sufferings that he endured? He replied that his desire to help souls suffering on this earth made his own sufferings seem mild in comparison. But what enabled him to *desire* to be of such service? His love for God, said Teresa. This is the root of all love; from here stems our love for our neighbors and the true love of self.

In our self-focused world, how do we shift our attention to the greater truth? We have created an intricate web of boundaries, which are based on people's occupations, personal interests, skills and abilities, race, color, religion, and so on. As long as we are separating ourselves from one another in this way, we remain within the smaller context of life, making the shift to a greater reality difficult. When we are able to dissolve these boundaries, then we will truly be free; only then will we disengage from separation and enter the larger picture of humanity, automatically awakening our desire to be of service. With this awakening we too will be able to endure our mission with greater ease, and we will join the masters who have walked before us in creating a better world to live in.

Our personal life, of course, is still relevant; however, now it can come into a balanced perspective, with both our life and the world taking on a new quality. We will find compassion for the person next to us, no matter what he believes, no matter what causes her pain. We are not just living for the "I" anymore; we are living for the "We," in the broadest possible sense.

Meditation

Taking yourself into your inner sanctuary, let your soul come to a deep peace. Ask to be shown areas in your life where boundaries still exist — old prejudices or judgmental beliefs — and know they are no longer necessary. Ask that you be taken into the larger context of your life and that of all humanity. Lay yourself down in this matrix of love and compassion.

45. Transforming the Silkworm

*When the soul is, in this prayer, truly dead to the world,
a little white butterfly comes forth. (CW vol. II, 343)*

BEING AWARE of the transformational process we have
embarked on with our desire to know both God and
ourselves, we now consciously enter and become fully
engaged in the mystical realities of our life. These realities present themselves to us daily through learning
experiences and personal revelations, and consequently
we are *altered* in miraculously small and large ways. We
finally come to understand and acknowledge that a
force larger than us is at work, preparing and fashion-
ing us according to the divine desire. We come to
know that we are nothing without this loving hand,
and *everything* with it. Our humility is being born
anew. We are being transformed in ways that we would

never have considered possible, and we begin to realize that God lovingly watches every step we take.

Teresa compared our journey with the process of the silkworm. Beginning as small grubs, they come to life only when the mulberry leaves appear, nourishing themselves on these leaves and growing into full-sized worms. Settling on twigs, they begin spinning their silken cocoon, in which they enclose themselves. In time the worm dies, and a pretty butterfly is born. Teresa recapitulated the spiritual journey, describing how our true life begins when we acknowledge our spirit-self and we nourish it with reading, meditation, and prayer. Through this nourishment we become ready to spin our own silken house, that is, the dwelling place of God. In this house, we die to our life as we have previously known it, and in time, as with the silkworm, we emerge as the butterfly, ready to fly out into the world.

Teresa believed that at this point the butterfly, even though it is experiencing a quietness and calmness of the soul for the first time, is still restless. It desires to fly wherever it can, using its new skills; it is no longer happy to crawl. However, it feels agitated because it is not sure where it should alight and flits about with uncertainty. The soul has been born anew and is no longer satisfied with its efforts in the world. It now wants to bring its new awareness to its daily life in a larger way, but is unsure about how to do so. It feels an urgent desire to be of use. The poor little butterfly, said Teresa: where is it to go? It cannot return to its cocoon;

all it can do is to wait on God, and it is not to be dismayed if it once more seeks rest, for when the time is right, its wings will work effortlessly.

As we awaken from our cocoon and find our wings, let us not be in too big a hurry to use them. Our only urgent need is to listen for the voice of God to direct us. And if we sometimes have to wait to hear it, then so be it; let us not fret over our feelings of uncertainty. We waste too much time and energy in this way, and then we create such a cacophony in our head that we are unable to hear God's voice when He *does* talk to us. Rather, let us use this time wisely to replenish our energy, and let us be gentle with ourselves in the process. Our wings are always there, and always will be. There is no beginning and no end in this wondrous game of love.

Meditation

Feel yourself in your cocoon, then gently let yourself emerge into the light. Do not be in a hurry, but let yourself slowly unfold in your own time. Feel the gentle freedom of your self being born — no need to take to the skies — and simply bask in the light of love and be wholly present in your new dwelling place.

46. God's Generosity

*He would never want to do anything else than give
if He could find receivers. (CW vol. II, 250)*

IN OUR SOCIETY, the ability to receive is an underde-
veloped art. We all need to be reeducated in this area,
particularly when it comes to receiving from God.
Teresa believed that God keeps nothing from us, and so
we need to seriously ask the question, Who is stopping
God's flowing generosity, and why?

Throughout our lives many resistances can build up
without our realizing it. They may be caused by professional disappointments or personal rejections creating a deep internal hurt and anger, which we may or
may not express. If we do not deal with the root cause
sufficiently, and if we do not release and heal the issue,
very often we start to resent God. And because it is not

"religiously correct" to be resentful of God, we avoid the issue and continue on, with our soul slowly smoldering. We might also start to resent God if we harbor anger over world issues, such as hunger, war, or environmental disasters. Lurking below the surface, more often than not, is a feeling of incredulity over how God could let these things happen. We may also have trouble understanding how God could create a people capable of such atrocities.

Whatever the cause of our anger or resentment, personal or universal, the reason and the result are the same. That is, we are disagreeing with God, and in doing so we are creating a wall of resistance that keeps God out. We may think that events should be happening in a different way, and we may have our own agenda about when they should happen. Teresa believed that the soul becomes extremely anguished when God's timing differs from its own. Even if what takes place is for the greater good of all, and divine guidance has assured the soul of this, we still may feel uncomfortable if what happens is not what we anticipated. The poor soul, said Teresa, how it grieves over this apparent delay. She came to see, however, that this grieving was unnecessary and gave up on her own plans, asking God to show her "where, how, and when." That is, she surrendered to where she was to be, how it was to occur, and when it would happen. She opened her soul to receive all that God wanted to give her, and so He did, giving her an exquisite taste of divine grace working *through* her and *for* her, at every moment that she was ready to receive.

Teresa maintained that it is imperative at this stage of our journey not to fall into doubt about God's willingness to help us. She said that God *needs* us to desire His favors so that we may receive them and bring them into the world for all to see. If we are still bound to our own plans or fettered by our unresolved anger toward God, then we are not only denying God's grace, but we are also slowing down the universal process of human spiritual evolution. Ultimately, God desires both our personal and universal evolution. We must learn to accept that they will occur in God's way, time, and place, which is here and always now. That is, what is occurring *now* in your life is God revealing and giving Himself to you. Are you willing to receive?

Meditation

Bless yourself and your life. Breathe into your existence. Let any feelings of resistance arise — let them come forward and speak. Ask God to help you in accepting what has occurred. Ask for greater acceptance in your life and in the world around you, and open yourself to receive the many blessings that God is waiting to give you.

47. The Meeting

*It is all a union of love with love... entirely pure,
and so delicate and gentle... there is no way
of describing [it]. (IC, 119)*

THE CONCEPT OF SPIRITUAL UNION often occupies a very lofty position, relegated only to saints and enlightened beings. For most of us, entering into union is understood as far beyond our reach, and any thought of obtaining it is quickly shrouded in feelings of unworthiness. Teresa, however, did not share this perspective. She believed there to be varying degrees of union that we can *all* experience as we travel into the interior of our castle. And if we keep our faces turned toward God, He can take us into the deepest union of love, both known and unknown, on this earth. It is we who place the limits on where we can travel, not God.

Teresa described one state of union as a "meeting,"

using the analogy of two people attracted to one another and coming together in love. Although they entertain the serious notion of marriage, they must continue to meet to better appreciate each other and to see if they are well suited. If they continue to love, they become betrothed and prepare for their wedding. So it is between the soul and God. We feel the desire to come together in the human-divine partnership of love, and God seeks to show Himself with even greater clarity and depth. If the soul continues to surrender, the meeting occurs. There is no giving or taking in this meeting, that is, there is nothing to be done or asked for; there is only a unity of being. The soul now sees the One it is going to accept on an even deeper level. The way in which the soul sees God is a secret, said Teresa, and all our senses and faculties could not in a thousand years understand what it has been given in this moment of union. All the soul knows is that it is "fired with love" and that it wishes to become betrothed, or committed to the divine, in a way it has previously not felt.

This meeting can occur anytime that God wishes it to. Preparing ourselves through constant self-surrender is our task; this task brings us to the ultimate joy of union, even if only experienced for a short time. The implications of this unity cannot be expressed adequately in words; our lives can only become a living testimony to the way our souls have been touched. God has ignited our own divine love. *We are love uniting with love.* And through the purity of this experience, we are now able to open to others, filled as we are with the same gentleness and tenderness that God has shown us. We become very deeply conscious of the love that lives within us and its gentle qualities; we can offer them to all we meet, no matter how different personalities may collide.

We are asked to surrender our defensiveness, which we all have and which is usually placed there for self-preservation. It is now no longer necessary, since the only thing we need to preserve is this gift of divine love. We are blessed to know this union. Let us accept it gratefully and use it wisely for the advancement of our soul and for the good of all.

Meditation

Breathe into your own love. Let any feeling of defensiveness rise. See how you may attack others, and ask why. Know that this is no longer necessary and ask to be released from this behavior. Let yourself surrender into the natural state of your own gentle being. Allow the divine love to meet you. Be in this love.

Sixth Dwelling

THE BETROTHAL

*We are already betrothed and before the wedding must
be brought to His house. (CW vol. II, 124)*

Through surrendering ourselves to the divine we are invited to enter the deep inner chambers where the betrothal between the soul and God occurs. Teresa warned, however, that in this dwelling we need more courage than we think. This is also the house where a deep and refined purification takes place and where the dark night of the soul may be experienced.

In this dwelling we will be confronted by all that remains to separate us from God; whatever still survives in our soul from past wounds and ego desires will emerge to be cleansed. We may also be left to walk alone on this part of the journey, not feeling the presence of God or having human support. However, in traveling through this purifying crucible we will come to know the art of detachment and the purity of humility.

It is with love and courage that we make our way into the sixth dwelling.

48. Wounded by Love

When the Gentle hunter
Wounded and subdued me,
In love's arms,
My soul fallen;
New life receiving,
Thus did I exchange
My Beloved is for me,
And I am for my Beloved. (CW vol. III, 379)

THE ARROW OF GOD'S LOVE never misses its target.
When we surrender our heart to the divine impulse it
becomes pierced by this arrow of love, and we desire to
be in the presence of our God as often as possible.
Teresa described this as a wounding of the soul, in
which a new and vehement love for the divine is born.
The soul does not fully comprehend what is occurring,
or how it has come to pass; all it knows is that it is
being called by God from deep within its own being.
It no longer wants to turn away or become involved
with distractions, since it is now aware that what is
being given is a precious gift. A new level of understanding is reached between the soul and God. Both

are preparing for the sacred marriage, and both are saying yes. This calling from God produces very delicate
and refined desires within the soul; it no longer feels
any urgency to be flying out in the world; rather, it
desires to be alone with God, since the soul wants only
to hear the divine voice. A new life is being given, and
a deeper intimacy is being entered into — the soul is
learning that God is its Beloved. The true betrothal has
begun, and the soul is filled with an even greater
yearning to be closer to its God. And herein lies the
paradox. The soul becomes consumed by desire for
the divine, and yet, there is nothing *to* desire, since the
soul is completely conscious of God's presence. This
yearning for the divine continues to be strongly felt,
however, and causes the soul to feel an internal pain
like nothing before experienced. But it is such an
exquisitely sweet pain, said Teresa, one that the soul
does not want to be relieved of, even if it could. It is as
if the tip of God's arrow carried the flame of divine
love, and when it pierces our soul we feel the fire deep
within. But when the arrow is removed, we are left
only with a spark, and so we yearn once more for the
flaming love. This action is very powerful, said Teresa;
it is the sweet spiritual pain of love that cannot be mis-
taken for anything other than God claiming the soul as
His own.

In our society, many have trouble with the concept
of paradox. Having been educated in linear thought
processes with rational deduction at the core, we find it
difficult to entertain the possibility that contradictory

thoughts can convey truth. And if we try to understand these paradoxical truths with our linear thinking, we will only confuse ourselves and alienate ourselves from God even more. If we wish to walk the spiritual pathway, Teresa believed, then we best learn, as quickly as possible, that contradiction is very often God's way. Do not expect God to walk a straight path, and do not expect to walk on one yourself. The map to love has many curves and circular roadways; learning this truth is a spiritual imperative.

When God's flaming arrow is aimed at our heart, let us not try to understand which bow He is using, or what types of arrows will affect us in different ways. Let us allow our souls to be pierced, and let us follow that spiritual wounding wherever it wants to take us. May we open our hearts fully and agree to become betrothed to the inner divine Beloved.

Meditation

Allow your soul to tenderly lie in the arms of love. Let all thoughts of how your life should be to fall from your mind. Allow all thoughts of how God should be to gently crumble. Open your soul to receive the life that God wants to give you. Open your heart to receive the Beloved. Speak the words with Teresa: "My Beloved is for me, and I am for my Beloved."

49. Purification

Lord, how You afflict Your lovers! But everything is small in comparison with what You give them afterward . . . it is as a small drop of water in the sea. (CW vol. II, 424)

ONCE WE HAVE PLEDGED OURSELVES in betrothal to the Beloved, a deep process of purification begins. It may feel as though we have been constantly purified as we have journeyed into this dwelling, and so we have. Now, however, impurities of our nature, and the lower impulses that have remained deeply embedded in our psyche, rise to greet us. We may be surprised at what emerges, not realizing that we were bound by these issues, or we may think that we had already dealt with them. These attachments may include old familial patterns of power and control, sexual desires for self-pleasure only, or old and undetermined anger resurfacing. These energies can be extremely powerful, and at times we may feel a sense of helplessness when they choose to visit us. At these times, it can also feel as if all our spiritual learning is lost in the torrent of their invasion and our subsequent behavior.

This is a crucial time in our spiritual development. We have been brought into the inner chambers of our own royal dwelling, where God has been generous in giving sweet delights to our soul. We have weathered the smaller trials of purification and tasted the joy of surrender, but now we are being called to endure the cleansing of the greater depths of our soul. We are being given the opportunity to be completely cleansed. For some, this process may be too demanding, since the soul has become accustomed to pleasures and to feelings of safety, even in the most restrictive psychological patterns and relationships. Others agree to the purification. Through remembering the *real* pleasure and joy experienced in surrendering to God, they are able to endure what is required, even with the absence of spiritual solace at the time.

Teresa described one of her experiences of purification as a time when her faith was deadened and put to sleep. It was as if she were spiritually numb; nothing pertaining to God could arouse even the slightest feeling within her, and the previous fervent love she had felt was barely lukewarm. Prayer was not only tedious but a torment to her, and no amount of effort could alleviate her situation. At these times, she experienced a ferocious anger: "I want to eat everybody up!" (*CW* vol. I, 259). At other times, she was incapable of thinking a single good thought, not about God or anybody else. She would then try to occupy herself with doing good works for others; however, since her soul was so lacking in grace, the works bore her dissatisfaction and distress only. No comfort was to be found anywhere. This is a trying time for the soul, she wrote, but once God lifts the soul from its misery, it feels like gold emerging from the crucible. The soul has a new purity and brightness, enabling it to see the hand of God in all that has passed. The soul emerges spiritually cleansed.

As we encounter our spiritual cleansing, we are given the choice to embrace the purification of our soul or to remain bound by the impulses of our nature. God does not judge what we choose; He simply invites us to keep progressing on our spiritual journey.

Meditation

Let yourself rest very deeply in your soul. Allow anything dwelling in the depths there to arise. See it and feel it. Decide if you want to keep what has arisen. If you wish it to be cleansed, ask for God's purifying love to come to you. Whatever your choice, let your journey continue.

50. Doubting God

*No matter how much I thought about this promise
I couldn't figure out how it would be possible, nor was
there a way of even imagining how it could come
about . . . but the means by which [it] eventually did
never entered my mind. (CW vol. III, 102)*

DOUBT IS ONE OF THE MOST COMMON STATES experienced by humanity, and it knows no discretion in
whom it chooses to afflict. We doubt ourselves, our
lovers, our workmates, and ultimately, we doubt the universal power of God. In this way, said Teresa, we stop the
magnificence of God working in our lives and fall back
into relying on ourselves to work out the solutions. If
we did not doubt, the solution would automatically be
supplied, but this concept is difficult for the mind to
fully grasp. Being a people of little patience, we demand
the answer now and are not prepared to wait for the
natural unfolding of the situation. "Wait a little, daughter, and you will see great things" (*CW* vol. III, 102).

These words were divinely spoken to Teresa, as she prayed for guidance in her destined vocation as reformer of the Order. Six months later, she began to witness the *beginning* of this fulfillment.

This decree for her vocational life, though divinely supported, was not without enormous struggles and trials. For some reason, Teresa said, the soul experiences great confusion and pain when divine guidance is not fulfilled according to its expectation. She experienced this often. At times, all things — people, money, and whatever else she needed — would seem to divinely flow. At other times, however, everything seemed to go wrong: houses promised would be withdrawn at the last minute; church prelates would present obstacles; or towns and other religious orders would resent the arrival of Teresa and her nuns. On one occasion she arrived with six other nuns in the town of Medina at midnight, only to be greeted by the sight of a very dilapidated house. Most of the walls had fallen to the ground, and there were openings onto the street. With little money they could not rent other accommodations or begin repairs. They had no alternative but to wait on the grace of God.

Teresa was deeply disturbed by these and other similar occurrences. Having been divinely guided she would begin to question her actions and ask, "Who got me involved in all this?" (*CW* vol. I, 312). Very quickly she would forget all the divine assurance she had previously received and was aware only of the predicament she was now faced with. She would torment herself with trying to think how she could rectify the situation, but ultimately, as always, God would send help in the most unlikely fashion, in His own way and time. For instance, after Teresa and her nuns had stayed for eight days in the dilapidated house in Medina, help came through the generosity of an unknown businessman. The new convent was created as God had promised.

Teresa wrote that these times of waiting for God were the most difficult periods in her life, and she would experience great anguish and also depression. She would question other directives she had received for the future: were they also in danger of not coming to fruition, and was her guidance all an illusion? Sometimes it would take years for things to come to fulfillment, but with the continual occurrence of these experiences, her faith was strengthened. The contradictions she encountered came to mean very little to her. This was the great learning, she said. We too can learn from her, and from our own experiences, by relinquishing our doubts and allowing God's love to be fulfilled.

Meditation

Come into your place of stillness and settle there with peace and ease. Let any doubts from deep within arise. See how they affect your faith and your life. What do you have doubts about? Bring these doubts into the realm of love, and relinquish them to God.

51. Courage

Sometimes the soul feels, and in the smallest things, that it is a coward, and so timid and frightened it doesn't think that it has the courage to do anything. (CW vol. II, 393)

As WE ENTER DEEPER into the purification process, we will also be faced with any fears that have been residing in the recesses of our psyche, and sometimes we are asked to face these fears alone. Even though we may have support from our partners and our community, at times we will be called to walk on our path unaccompanied and unsupported by others. This is not an easy task and takes courage, since we must follow our own inner calling and discernment and not rely on others to confirm that we are acting in the right way. To walk alone can be a frightening experience, but essentially we are all walking on our own unique path. By not seeking or gaining validation from others, we build an inner strength that can be used in the unfolding of our divine purpose. Ultimately, we are being asked to follow the command of God over reliance on our human companions.

Teresa said she experienced times of great courage when she felt that she would not turn from anything that was clearly of service to God. Her soul was strong and acted on her inner conviction without any concern at all; these were times when she made great strides for God's work on earth. And then on other days, she felt that she had not the courage to do anything at all. Even the slightest opposition from another would cause her great distress and leave her with a feeling of helplessness and an inability to act. How tiny and desperate the soul feels at these times, she said, since it is clearly not in a position to achieve anything, not for its own good or for the good of others. And even when we turn to others for direction, we may find no solace, since their words may be either harsh or not relevant to the soul's distress. This is when a feeling of deep loneliness and the fear that we will always be alone on our spiritual journey can arise. Other deep-seated fears can also arise, attacking our self-confidence or our judgment about our mental health and well-being. This can be further exacerbated if we are experiencing physical illness, fatigue, depression, or anxiety, which are not uncommon during the time of purification. Teresa mentions how she could barely lift her pen at such times, and she was often bedridden during her greatest cleansings.

We may also come to question whether we truly wish to continue on the path we have chosen. We may yearn for the old life lived in ignorance of the reality we are now being shown. It is as if we are living in a place of transition where a decision is pending: should we leave our old life behind completely, or should we turn back from the journey we have embarked on? When we do not find solutions in others' words, the responsibility of the answer lies solely in us. A paradox is at play here. By coming to the One who is calling us, we must gather up all our own courage. Yet in doing so, we are also gifted with a courage of divine proportions that enables many wonderful and miraculous things to occur on our journey. In letting go of our life as we have known it, we are now given the life that has been divinely arranged for us.

By remaining in the constancy of God's love, said Teresa, all can be conquered. And that is exactly what is occurring; God is conquering the soul's deepest fears to take us fully into the realm of love.

Meditation

Let yourself come into the light of God's love. Allow the deepest fears of the soul to emerge — speak them to God in full honesty. Ask for the courage needed to give over everything to Him; you no longer need to hold on to anything. You are safe in love.

52. Divine Loss

To this life
Worldly love adheres;
Love divine
For the other sighs.
Eternal God, without You,
Who can live? (CW vol. III, 383)

SEPARATION IS THE ESSENTIAL CAUSE of grief on this planet. By experiencing separation from our divine source, we also come to see ourselves as separate from one another, whether it be through difference in culture, religion, or species. Our spiritual history is and has been a slow process of evolution. It is bringing us back into a place of unity — with our divine source, with ourselves, and with others. An acutely dire but seemingly necessary experience for our spiritual growth entails coming into complete consciousness of the separation. By doing so, we open the way for the unity to occur. This dynamic is found among most mystics and is known as the "dark night of the soul." Many people today are living in a state of separation without conscious awareness of doing so. They are also unaware of the light of unity that awaits them. Conversely, those entering the final purification know that there is *always* light after loss.

Teresa was a woman who felt intensely, and so her experiences of darkness, or the feelings of divine absence, were excruciating for her. She wrote that it feels as if God has rejected the soul, as if the soul knows nothing but separation, with no remedy available. There is nowhere for the soul to alight, since it can touch neither earth nor heaven, and it is left as if suspended, with a consuming thirst that cannot be quenched. The soul knows that the only water able to give relief is the water spoken of by Jesus to the Samaritan woman, but it is denied. It is in and through this agony, however, that the gift of knowledge comes. And this is the knowledge that separation from God is the only real grief that we experience here on earth. All our fears and feelings of fragility and inadequacy come from this feeling of separation. All our prejudices and judgments arise because we think we are separate. When we consciously know this separation to be the cause of our many anxieties and difficulties, it becomes easier to allow a final purification of the will to occur. We are being prepared for a complete unification with God.

We may experience divine loss when it appears that nothing is going well in our lives, when we feel no connection to ourselves or to God, or when our fellow human companions sorely test us. These experiences may occur simultaneously, or consecutively, and like Teresa, we may feel abandoned by God with no immediate remedy apparent. Her advice is to engage in external works of love, no matter what feelings arise, and to know that the light of God will shine once more on your soul when the time is right.

The dark night of the soul can be a time when people become lost and return to their old ways of living, forgetting the love that previously shone in their hearts. Or it can be a time of moving into a more mature spirituality. Love for God is no longer only about joyful emotions but is a true surrender of self. A sense of selflessness, and an ability to love for love's sake alone, is born.

Let us join with the mystics in learning that we *all* come from the same divine source and that we can all actively participate in bringing a message of peace to our world through our daily living.

Meditation

Bless your life and soul as they are. Thank God for everything that comes your way. Notice any feelings of separation you may have — between you and God, between you and others. Ask that you may come into the eternal truth of unity, and bless all that lives.

53. Patience

Let nothing disturb you,
Let nothing frighten you
Everything passes,
God does not change,
Patience
Everything does obtain. (AT, CW vol. III, 386)

IN OUR GOAL-ORIENTED SOCIETY often we give
precedence to our goals, with little regard for the
process required to reach them. Sometimes, in hind-
sight, we may see the value in the steps taken; at other
times we are already on our way to the next goal. We
can easily fall into this predicament on our spiritual
journey, hastily making our way to the top of the
mount without valuing the gradual ascent or God's
way of leading us. As we journey through this sixth
dwelling, we may be tempted to speed up the process,
to get this purification over and done with. However,
these are very important steps and must be taken in
God's time and not ours.

Teresa spoke very clearly about attempting to meddle with God's ways, and she related how she would pray for her trials to cease, until she realized what great gifts were being given to her through those trials. If we try to free ourselves from the darkness we are encountering, we are halting our soul's process; even if this darkness sometimes includes bodily pain, it can be a doorway to a wonderful purification. But be careful also about asking for *more* purifying, Teresa advised, since we may be opening a door that we are not yet ready to walk through. Do not hasten the process or try to deter it. For in doing so, we are essentially stating that we know better than God.

When she was young, Teresa would complain to God, saying, "Oh, Lord, I didn't want so much" (*CW* vol. II, 251). But she would be given such strength and patience that even years later she was amazed at her fortitude. We should thank God, she believed, for it is He who delivers and grants the patience when required. And He calls so unexpectedly, with a word or thought that calms the storm and clears the clouds from the soul. We cannot know how long our trials will last — sometimes they will last days, sometimes months or years — but with God-given patience *all* can be endured. The most valuable lesson, said Teresa, is that God alone does all. The soul need no longer reflect on what it should do. This is very important preparation, she said, for what lies ahead of us on our journey.

Patience and compassion are like sister and brother. Feeling deeply into our own dark nights, we can enter into a selfless appreciation of others and their times of spiritual desolation. We can allow them the space to purify their souls and bodies as required. And in knowing that we cannot quicken our own process, we understand that other people are exactly where God wants them to be as well. We can allow them the necessary time to cleanse. After all, who are we to meddle with their destined journey?

As Ecclesiastes says, "There is a season for everything...a time for giving birth, a time for dying...a time for tears, a time for laughter...a time for losing, a time for keeping" (3:2–6).

May we use our understanding and the gift of patience to accept all God's blessings.

Meditation

Bringing yourself into the center of your being, feel any resistance you may have to allowing your process to unfold in its own way and time. Identify what lies beneath these resistances, and take them to God. Ask that you may be granted the patience needed to walk your journey as divinely intended — and wait for God's reply.

54. Abandoning to Love

Give me wealth or want,
Delight or distress,
Happiness or gloominess,
Heaven or hell, . . .
Sweet life, sun unveiled,
To You I give all. (CW vol. III, 378)

WITH THE CONTINUED PRACTICE OF PATIENCE, the soul learns the art of detachment. It no longer becomes lost in the myriad of thoughts that invade the mind but instead recognizes God speaking to it *through* these thoughts. In the light of this recognition the soul is now able to forgo self-judgment. So quickly we put ourselves down, and in doing so, we annihilate the divine messenger before the message is even heard. Through surrendering our thoughts to God, we can let Him in anytime He wants to visit. We can then slowly identify with the inner God-self, enabling the ego to transcend any attachments, conceptual or actual. We are being called to abandon the frameworks we have created — the personal and the societal, the religious and the spiritual — in an attempt to make us feel safe.

Teresa's words above very eloquently speak to this kind of abandonment. She has relinquished any desire for her own state of mind or being; her position in society is of no consideration, and her spiritual gains are no longer relevant. She moves into a delightful place of equanimity where all states are accepted equally. However, she goes beyond acceptance and now finds great joy in whatever is given to her. This is how patience grows: we begin by grudgingly accepting our situation, then we move to a place of neutrality, and in time we rejoice over every message delivered to us. It is the ego, after all, that complains, not the spirit. As our identification with the God-self strengthens, we come to know, with absoluteness, that the divine flame is purifying us for our highest good.

Teresa reminds us of the Lord's prayer (Matthew 6:10), which she wrote as "Your kingdom come within us" (*CW* vol. II, 150). She maintained that we are given this kingdom here on earth while we are still alive, and that we will find it *within*. By understanding the great relevance of this, she said, we come to see that the smaller earthly things that previously caused us concern no longer bind us. The soul then falls into a feeling of tranquillity, no matter what it experiences. It now feels only a love for the ways of God and wants to give all of itself. The soul has come to implicitly trust God and walks with clarity in the light with which it now identifies.

In *Mysticism: The Nature and Development of Spiritual Consciousness,* Evelyn Underhill writes, "When all forms have ceased to exist, in the twinkling of an eye the man is transformed...entering even further in" (400). We abandon, says Underhill, old modes of perceiving, permitting movement toward the new Transcendental Self. This new Self permeates more and more of our personality and sinks deeper into the unknown. So it was with Teresa's journey, and so it can be with ours. We no longer need to seek safety by binding ourselves to outdated forms and theories. Releasing them, we can step safely into the universal unknown — finding the fullness of ourselves within the emptiness of our being.

Meditation

Coming into your inner sanctum of peace, allow a deep calm to enter your soul. See what form you identify with — your role at work or at home, or your spiritual beliefs — and lay them aside. Let yourself sink deeper into your divine self, releasing anything that may bind you. Slowly lower yourself even more into your depths — letting go of any fear, knowing that you are safe in the universal love — and breathe, breathe into the unknown of your own delightful being.

55. True Humility

Here true humility can enter the picture because this virtue and the virtue of detachment it seems to me always go together. They are two inseparable sisters. (CW vol. II, 76)

THE TRUTH OF HUMILITY is found in our understanding and acknowledgment of the supreme reality of our existence, that is, that we are all manifestations of God. He is the flame, and we are the sparks of His divine love, created in the purity of His being. To be humble means to know and honor our origins. It also means to remember, at all times, that it is through the very love of God that we live and breathe and journey through this life. We are being asked to live these supreme and everlasting truths, said Teresa, even though we know so little about this majestic sovereignty of the divine being.

There are stages to be recognized as we learn about humility, and, as Teresa put it, we should seek to draw out the truth in everything, thus coming to know what is false and what is real. When we are still attached to our ego, we will pass through two particular phases: in the first, we will desire praise and recognition, hoping for our own wisdom to be acknowledged; and in the second, we will wish *not* to be recognized at all, we will seek to hide from the world, yet we will still secretly harbor the desire to be seen. As we move deeper into detachment from the ego-self and the world's expectations, we move into a place of indifference. This occurs, said Teresa, as we realize that though people say both good and bad things about us, when we are detached, these things will have no effect on us. We will feel no desire either to be seen or not to be seen. The final stage expands the soul until it reaches a completely new understanding. Here it comes to fully honor God by acknowledging that its being is completely reliant on Him for *everything.* When we make this ultimate humility a living reality, other souls are able to see the work of God's blessing in us. This brings great joy to the truly humble soul. In this final stage, we delight in knowing that it is God's truth, not us, being praised.

Just as detachment is necessary before we can experience true humility, so is the virtue of love. Teresa says there cannot be humility without love, or love without humility. If we love someone we do not raise ourselves above him or her. By humbling ourselves, said Teresa, we draw love and peace into our souls; in this way, when we are walking with humility, God will give us everything of Himself. But when we are without humility, He will leave us to our own devices, so that we may learn about our true nature.

We are asked to walk on the pathway of supreme truth with God *and* our fellow human beings. When we are humble before God but not with our neighbor we cannot create a living truth. And if we proclaim to love God but do not love our neighbor, then we are living a lie. As St. Paul said, though you may possess all the spiritual gifts, without love they are as nothing (1 Corinthians 13:1–13). God, love, humility, and our fellow beings are all of the same divine nature; when we come to fully understand and live this reality we will have entered a minute part of the supreme truth.

Meditation

Come into your place of deep quiet. Examine the ways in which you may raise yourself above others or desire recognition for yourself. Lay them at the feet of love. Ask that true humbleness may enter your soul, and let your ego dissolve in the gift of love and true humility. Let your being expand into the smallness and grandness of your own nature.

56. Divine Madness

> *Let Him kiss me with the kiss of His mouth*
> *for His breasts are better than wine, and give forth*
> *the most sweet fragrance. (Song of Songs 1:2–3)*

A COMMON EXPERIENCE FOR MYSTICS is relating to God as their lover. Not only by loving but also by *falling in love* with God, they fall into a deep rapturous love with all of life. Everywhere they look this love is to be found, and it feels to them as if they have literally fallen into a huge ocean of love. This ecstatic experience is not relegated to the chosen few; rather, it is available to all who are able to give themselves totally to God by walking, in truth, through *all* the dwellings. Teresa said that as she passed through the trials demanded of her, she began to feel much stronger impulses of love. She also experienced, during these times, much deeper raptures in communion with God. Again, she reminds us that not only she but also many other nuns and also priests knew of these great secrets of God.

We are not to be shy, she said, when it comes to loving our God. Let us demand that He love us as the bridegroom loved his Beloved in the Song of Songs. And let us respond with equal ardor. To receive the divine kiss, she said, is the ultimate gift — it is at once a rapturous delight and the deepest divine peace. For Teresa, this experience could come at any time. In fact, one needs courage for this experience, she said, since one is taken in spirit very rapidly to a place unknown and unsought by the soul. One may experience fear at first, since there is no warning and one has no idea of what is occurring. Only when it is revealed that it is God taking it on this wondrous journey does the soul learn to implicitly trust in this divine action. The effects on the soul are profound, said Teresa: such an intensity of sweetness is felt that both the body and the soul are left in a state of wonder that seems to temporarily paralyze them. "It seems to the soul it is left suspended in those divine arms, leaning on the sacred side and those divine breasts" (*CW* vol. II, 244). Teresa believed that the soul is incapable of anything except rejoicing in the splendor and the "divine milk" that nourishes it. When it emerges from this state the soul is inflicted with a "holy madness" and appears completely drunk. The soul is filled with a joy so excessive that it wants to let the whole world know about the greatness of God.

There also comes, however, a very profound realization, and the soul feels as though it has finally found itself, that its long search is finally over. The betrothal in its entirety has now occurred, and there can be no denying that the sacred marriage will take place. The Beloved has arrived to claim the soul, and with this comes absolute safety; the soul is literally falling into the arms of God and of love.

The ecstatic joining of two lovers spreads delight across the universe. The joining of God and soul cannot be measured. To participate in this great adventure of love with God can only bring goodness to all — we need only the courage and faith to continue loving and to allow ourselves to be continually loved. We are all the chosen people of God, and everything that He offers is available to each of us. Let us not deny Him the opportunity to love us as He desires.

Meditation

Coming deep into the interior of your being, allow your body and soul to be surrendered completely to God. Feel your breath become the divine breath. Feel your heartbeat become the divine heartbeat. Allow yourself to be taken by the divine love deep into the source of your being. Let yourself be loved in any way that God desires.

Seventh Dwelling

THE SACRED MARRIAGE

*It detaches itself from everything . . . so as to abide
more in me. It is no longer the soul that lives
but I. (CW vol. I, 163)*

The seventh dwelling is the place of union. The soul, having emptied itself of *itself,* now comes into the purity of its own divine and human being. It is not a place of constant heavenly rapture, but a joining of the worlds, making the divine Word incarnate in and through everyday actions. It is the constant remembrance of our inner God.

In this, the final dwelling, we are asked to celebrate our lives: our work, our relationships, and our play. Through perceiving the presence of God in everything and everybody, the soul is now free to live in the unity it has always inherently known.

Here the journey does not end but only truly begins.

57. Union of the Human and Divine

*In the spiritual marriage the union is like . . .
when rain falls from the sky into a river . . . all is water,
for the rain that fell from heaven cannot be divided
or separated from the water or river. (CW vol. II, 434)*

AS WE BEGAN OUR SPIRITUAL JOURNEY we were awoken to another reality that had been waiting for us, a truth that beckoned us to move beyond separation. Our relationship with this divine truth took us in and out of different states of consciousness, as it commanded and as we allowed. At times we experienced union with this divine source, and at other times we felt a definite sense of disconnection. Now, in this seventh dwelling, there is no more separation, and we need no longer fear ever being separated again from the divine love that forever abides within. Something occurs within the soul that allows it to transcend even a "knowing" of this truth. The soul is now entering *a state of being* in which the divine love is fulfilled and in which the soul is not only given *to* God, but it is surrendered *in* God. This is the sacred or spiritual marriage.

Teresa received the grace of this marriage thirty-seven years after she entered the monastery, and ten years before her death. She had just received communion when she heard these words from deep within: "Don't fear, daughter, for no one will separate you from Me...you will be My bride from today on... My honor is yours, and yours Mine" (*CW* vol. II, 402). She described how this secret union occurred in the deepest center of her soul and that it had the most profound effect on her; it revealed that this was where God Himself was dwelling. This union, she said, was unlike the feelings of unity or rapture experienced in the fifth or sixth dwellings. In these previous dwellings the separation always came again, even though the soul had been radically transformed. Here, in the seventh dwelling, the soul remains with its God; it does not move again from here, its very center of being. The two now become merged into one. Just as betrothed couples join to create a life together upon marrying, so too does the soul join with God to participate in the one life.

The soul experiences great confidence through this union, said Teresa, since it knows in the most interior part of its being that God is dwelling there and that He will never leave. The soul marvels at this; Teresa maintained that there is no way to describe the difference between *hearing* about this indwelling of God and actually *experiencing* it. Teresa acknowledged that she had been given the greatest gift of all — eternal divine companionship. She lived the next ten years of her life in and with this glorious company.

The consummation of our journey, the sacred marriage, is the ultimate union to be experienced by each soul. By following the commands of our deepest self we will experience the same divine company that Teresa enjoyed. We will come to live in unity with the divine source; there will be no more separation, or the accompanying fears of this falsely perceived state. The inner divine self will finally have the freedom to express the love and purity of its essential being and consciousness.

Meditation

Bring yourself into a place of deep quiet. Allow yourself to settle there. Notice any fears about being separated from the divine source. Bring them to God. Ask that you may be free from such fears or any other feelings keeping you apart. Allow the unity of being to touch your soul and spirit. Bless this unity in yourself, in the world around you, and in the creative universal force that brings all into the sacredness of life.

58. Perceiving the Presence

From within my soul — where I saw these three Persons present — these persons were communicating themselves to all of creation without fail. (CW vol. II, 393)

THE MYSTERIES OF GOD ARE INFINITE, and there is none so mystifying as the doctrine of the Trinity. We have Christ, who manifests the divine spirit in and through the human form; the Holy Spirit, who is present in every being and is guiding and inspiring us at every moment; and the Creator Spirit, who gave us this life. These are all distinct forces, and yet they are one, just as we are all different beings and yet joined, with each other *and* with this Trinitarian spirit of creation. The experience of the Trinity may come in various forms, as attested to by other religions, and need not necessarily be described only in Christian terminology. When we enter the grand mystery of the spirit, it takes us far beyond any doctrine or theory. Teresa spoke with awe as she searched for words to describe her experience and the knowledge she was given.

She wrote about how God now removes the scales from the soul's eyes, allowing it to see and understand things that it previously was unable to comprehend. A profound truth about the nature of the three Persons is revealed. All three communicated to her in such a way that she knew they were distinct yet also one substance and one power. They also communicate with one another, she said, and love and know one another as the one essence. Nothing can be achieved without all three acting together as one. Later, as she reflected on this experience, her mind tried to conceptually grasp the reality of what her soul had witnessed. Very quickly she was told by God that the ways of this world are very different from that of the spirit and that it was futile to make any comparisons.

Teresa was also made aware that all three Persons dwelled within her own being. She described this as the Trinity "bearing an imprint in her soul," with no separation between her and the three Persons. Even though this realization lasted only a moment, she said she benefited from it far more than she did from many years of meditation. She no longer believed in the Trinity through faith, but through knowledge deep within her soul. She says that whenever she thought of Christ, she now also thought of the Holy Spirit and the Creator; they were inseparable — just as she was from them.

Christ came to show us our ability to walk on this earth as both human and divine beings. He taught that just as He is in the Father and the Father is in Him (John 14:11), so it is with all of creation. He also said that the very spirit of God is the messenger of truth that we can all receive (John 16:13). This is the Trinitarian unity of love. Fortunately, people like Teresa and others are able to realize this unity, and their lives continue to remind us of this truth. May we all receive the encouragement that we need to travel on our spiritual pathway, and may we come to know and live the Trinitarian aspect of our being.

Meditation

Breathe into the very spirit of your being. Allow yourself to feel the essence of this spirit. Feel how this spirit is joined with the divine Creator. Feel how it is joined with you. Open yourself to receive whatever is given.

59. True Love

*Those whom God brings to a certain clear knowledge
love very differently... this clear knowledge is about the
nature of the world, that there is another world... that
the one is eternal and the other a dream. (CW vol. II, 62)*

OUR WORLD IS BESOTTED WITH LOVE. No matter
where we turn — to popular or religious culture, or to
psychological or new age theories — love is the key
factor. We are all searching and yearning for love,
whether to replace a love lost or to find a love never
before felt. Most people have a place deep within that
is aching to be loved. Some acknowledge this, some
bury it in their work or addictions, while others are
disappointed with the love they are experiencing. Love
entices us all, and yet it seems to elude us just as easily.
What is this thing called love? Where is the true love
that many of us instinctively know exists? For most, it
has been relegated to an unrealistic dream world, as

practicality and dependency have overshadowed the realm of magic and aliveness felt when we first glimpse another's soul. Could it be that we have confused dream and reality and have settled for an illusory state of love? According to Teresa, this is so, and she reached out to remind us that clarity of being is necessary in understanding the true and perfect love.

Those who have been given knowledge of their true nature and of this world care little about being loved, Teresa said. Their only concern is for the soul of the other person. Love, for them, is only important when it is of spiritual benefit; all else is without substance. When we desire to have someone love us, we are seeking our own benefit or satisfaction, said Teresa. Our affections are blurred by our needs, and it is our own fulfillment that inspires the feelings that we mistake for love of the other. We suffer greatly, she believed, when these desires are not fulfilled. If another does fulfill them, also mistaking their feelings for love, we have a too-common scenario — two individuals in a codependent relationship, desiring their demands for love to be met. When we have clarity of perception we can see the illusion of such actions, and being unable to respond according to the other's desires, we may be accused of being unable to love. Yet the opposite is true.

It is impossible, said Teresa, for a soul who has surrendered itself to God to be intimately involved with another who is still attached to the mundane realm. That is, if one is still concerned with the wealth, reputation, or looks of another, this does not allow for true love to flourish. The perfection of love consists of traveling into the eternal realm of love where these things are no longer relevant (they may, Teresa said, still be enjoyed, but there is no attachment to them). In the realm of true love the clarity of being and vision come together as both people become a witness to each other's soul in the light of their spiritual well-being.

We are called, said Teresa, to imitate the love that Jesus, the good lover, had for us. Everything is seen and known in the truth of love; there is no false flattery or hiding anything from one another. In this way, lovers can advance far as they create an openness that allows them to soar toward God. Without the truth of love in our lives the soul can become weary; knowing this, God sends us a companion, in His own time, enabling us to enter into sincerity with ourselves and with others.

Meditation

Come into a place of deep being. Ask for clarity of vision. See what matters in your intimate relationships. See what your demands are. Is the spiritual welfare of your partner and yourself paramount? Ask to know the sincerity of your own soul.

60. Intimacy

*What a wonderful thing it is for two souls to understand
each other, for they neither lack something to say,
nor grow tired. (*Letters *no. 170:1, 450)*

OUR INTIMATE CONNECTIONS with our closest friends
are one of our greatest treasures and can give much solace to the soul. However, once the depth of intimacy
has been truly tasted, other types of relating may seem
pale in comparison. Even though we are destined to be
closer to some souls than to others, intimacy is ultimately about sincerity, and we *can* be sincere with
everybody, even with those we meet in the supermar-
ket. It is our duty to take the spark of love generated
through our close connections and spread it to all
we meet. Love cannot be guarded jealously, nor is it
a commodity to own. It is a light that needs to be
shared and to be given with generosity — just as it is

so generously given to us. We are the caretakers of this beautiful gift, and the more we share it with others, the more our soul becomes filled. It also gives others the opportunity to return to their own sincerity of soul — surely there can be no greater gift of love?

Teresa encouraged her nuns and priests to enter the depths of intimacy with one another at all times. She understood the great benefits derived from such intimate sharing, and she would openly reveal her soul to those she lived and worked with. She established deep and lifelong friendships, which were very important to her, and she did not refrain from speaking and showing the great affection and love she felt. Some priests were terrified of her candid behavior and believed her to be walking a very dangerous line. She would laugh to herself at their fear, since she knew they mistook the purity of her actions for something less elevated.

John of the Cross, though many years younger than Teresa, became her most intimate spiritual companion. She said she had "gone about here and there looking for light" and that she had found it in him (*Letters*, 642). They would spend many hours in conversation together, and the spiritual heights they reached were evident, since they physically levitated together, rising many feet into the air. She said that at times spiritual and sensual love become so intermingled, that no one can understand such love. She maintained that this is a completely normal occurrence between souls, whether male or female, and that there should be no torment over the great feeling of love that is aroused. If the soul is advancing toward God through this relationship, she advised, then let it continue. And if you find yourself becoming obsessed with thinking of the other person, then turn your thoughts back to God. She also warned, however, that if there was any lack of integrity, through conversation that led the soul away from God, then the association should cease.

Teresa advocated that intimacy was to be inclusive within her monasteries, that is, even though special friendships were formed, they should not leave others feeling excluded. Tenderness and affection should be displayed toward all, creating a loving communal atmosphere. Without this, she said, discord and isolation can easily arise, which was not the truth of the loving God that Teresa intimately knew. By taking these teachings into our everyday life, may we too practice the sincerity and tenderness of intimacy, with integrity and love, with all we meet.

Meditation

Breathe deeply into your most intimate being. Allow yourself to become fully immersed. Feel and explore this self. Love this self. Know your own tenderness — allow your natural affection to rise. Bring it forward into the world.

61. Passion of the Spirit

My heart is free
Causing a passion to well within me...
Afire in love's burning...
Life, what can I give? (AT, CW vol. III, 375–76)

PASSION HAS BEEN DEFINED as "ardent desire" or the state of being "moved by strong emotions." It is commonly associated with creative artistry in its many forms. It is also known to have a dark side, manifesting either as severe depression or as volatile mood swings. Repression of our passion, that is, of our strong feelings, can also cause violent outbreaks of emotion. This is seen only too clearly in domestic or work situations that we do not attend to when required. Psychologists have attempted to understand emotion through a lens of rationality. Theoretically this can work, but very often in the heat of the emotional moment, it just isn't enough.

Teresa asked whether we are to be ruled by our emotions or whether we are to be the ruler. She wrote that wherever emotions are present "good order is thrown into complete disorder" (*CW* vol. II, 57). She witnessed many "saintly" nuns become emotionally unraveled when their egos were put to the test. Their subsequent behavior attested to a passion of the ego rather than the passion of the spirit. Although these two passions are quite distinct, they are rarely differentiated in our world. When we remain attached to the ego's desires, our emotions quickly get the upper hand — either we become elated when the ego receives what it wants, or we become angry or depressed when it does not. The spirit is concerned with what it can give, not with what it can get; it is alight with the fire of God and feels a burning love for all beings. Its generosity becomes more and more apparent as it enters into life with passion, that is, with an ardent desire to fulfill its destiny in whatever way it is guided. As the soul becomes detached from expectations about its destiny, and how and with whom it is to evolve, it experiences freedom, in its truest sense. With this passion of spirit, we still strongly feel our emotions, only now they concern the benefit of all, not just that of the self.

It is interesting to remember that the last days of suffering in Christ's life are referred to as the Passion. Christ was so moved by the depth of his feeling and by his *passion* for humanity that he undertook and endured the most grueling destiny. This act is the epitome of the passion of the spirit. It takes us far beyond the explosive nature of the creative soul and leaves the rationale of psychological inquiry looking rather deficient. The true passion, the true spirit, enables God to live and work through the human and divine being.

Teresa wrote of how her emotions were finally conquered, which for the naturally passionate woman that she was, was probably no small feat. With humor, she added that her emotions now feared entering the center of the seventh dwelling, since they knew they would leave subdued. She was astutely aware of the difference between the two types of passion and gave herself with great desire to the One who could master all personal emotion. May we, when confronted with our own ego feelings, remember her humor and her passion and let these emotions pass us by.

Meditation

Bring yourself into the center of your being. Become a witness to your daily life and emotions. See how, and from where, your feelings emerge. Bring them into the light of your center. Ask that you be guided to connect with the passion of your spirit.

Let this guidance continue as you go about your daily tasks.

62. Martha and Mary

Although a person's life will become more active than contemplative... Martha and Mary never fail to work almost together when the soul is in this state. For in the active... the soul is working interiorly. (CW vol. II, 257)

CONTRARY TO POPULAR BELIEF, the pinnacle of the mystical life is often lived *in* the world, even though it is not *of* the world. Having come into a full consciousness of the reality of existence, the mystic is now returned to society, displaying an extraordinary energy for the work required. This energy is none other than the divine force working in and through this willing worker of God, and it far surpasses anything we human beings can do alone. Teresa's life is one such example of a person in and through whom God worked, and throughout her life she reiterated that the ultimate purpose of the sacred marriage is to give birth to good works in the world.

Many people today are confused about their spiritual purpose here on earth. Many feel impatient to begin what they perceive to be their destined work, but Teresa warns about "going out ahead of time" (*CW* vol. II, 260). We can damage both ourselves and others, she said, if we do not wait for God's direction. It is God who chooses what is required of us and when this will occur; we will not discover our work by thinking about it. As Teresa said, it is our job to love much and not to think much.

In the Book of Luke, Martha complains to Jesus that Mary is sitting there listening to Him and not helping with all the work that is being left to Martha alone. Jesus replied that Mary has chosen the better path (10:40). We are both Mary and Martha. First, we must remain open to hearing the words of God and to receiving them in the depths of our being; then we can act on these words. Sometimes no action will be required, and so we will remain with Mary. During these times Martha must learn to remain still. At other times we will become Martha, but always with Mary alongside to help with inner guidance. Teresa would complain that when she was attending to business affairs it was more difficult to remain aware of God's presence. She was told by God not to worry, since this is how it is, and that she must simply do her best. Encouraging words indeed in these times!

Teresa advised that we must be careful not to hide our talents. By emptying ourselves of who we think we are, we can join with the "uncreated Spirit" within.

Through this joining we can then give birth to possibilities and capacities that we never knew existed. We are no longer the person we were in our youth, and the dreams we once had for ourselves are no longer relevant. We are who we are now. We must not allow fears from our past to resurface and claim us.

It is not what we do, but how we do it, that matters, said Teresa. Each of us has a designated role to play on this earth, and when we enter into true harmony with our own being, this special place will be revealed to us. Be patient and know that "she who receives more serves more" (*CW* vol. II, 417).

Meditation

Come into your place of stillness and being. Breathe into this place and acknowledge how it serves you. See how it remains with you throughout the day, even when you are unaware of it. Bring your whole consciousness into its light. Open yourself to hearing the inner words of guidance, in all aspects of your life, and to act on them accordingly.

63. Remembering Your Humanness

It as an important thing that while we are living and are
human we have human support. (CW vol. I, 195)

ISOLATION IS A RARE FORM OF ASCETICISM practiced
by few today. The contemplative life, though struc-
tured to allow long periods of silence throughout the
day, is not actually dedicated to isolation, as many may
believe. The communal paradigm was created so that
support for members is constantly available for whatever needs may arise, be they physical, emotional, or
spiritual. By creating this supportive atmosphere, members can help one another in their chosen journeys of
love. We too are called to support one another in our
journeys, and we are also asked to receive that support
when we need it, in whatever form. In receiving graciously from another, without guilt or obligation, we

are opening the door of our own heart to give generously when it is needed. This kind of generosity is
marked by its purity; with our hearts open, we feel no
expectation of return or any judgment about the re-
quest. It will be as the support of a brother to a sister,
expressed with full integrity and love.

Teresa received much support from her fellow nuns
and priests as she traversed through the often rough ter-
rain of her life. When she was forced to come before
the Inquisition for her writings about her spiritual life
and experience, for example, Father Jerome Gracian, her
dear friend and confidant, was there to support her,
as he was many times throughout her life. He was also
of special help to her with the many administrative and
business matters she had to attend to. Teresa's love
and concern for him, and her deep gratitude to him,
were clearly indicated in the letters that she frequently
wrote to him when they were apart.

There was much resistance to the new Order from
the original Carmelite chapter, and Rome was oscillat-
ing in its support. The bureaucratic rulings in the Holy
See of Rome were often complex, and as the men in
power changed, so did their support for Teresa. She was
subjected to litigations against her, and many of her friars, including St. John of the Cross, were arrested and
imprisoned or exiled. She took counsel from both
Dominican and Jesuit priests during these times and
received enormous support for her work, even though
on her deathbed the controversies were still raging.

Ana de San Bartolomé, a young Carmelite nun

who humbly received the mystical and ecstatic graces, was Teresa's constant companion from 1577 to 1582, during which time a deep bond formed between the two women. Blessed Ana records the difficulties Teresa was subjected to: family dilemmas, problems in the monasteries, and poor health, right up to the time of her death. Ana supported her and did whatever she could to lighten her burden. It was in Blessed Ana's arms that Teresa died.

Teresa was adamant that the nuns should support one another in all their times of need and that they be especially compassionate toward those who were ill. Because of her own experiences, Teresa understood the great value of being loved and supported and was thus able to thoroughly love and support others. May we emulate her life, by loving others as we would be loved.

Meditation

Breathe into the blessings of your life. Feel how you would like to be supported. Are you open to receiving the love and support you desire without feeling obligated? Open your heart, and let the love of friends and family flow in to you. Let your own pure love flow out to those around you in need. Bless your life with gratitude.

64. Re-creation

Mother Foundress is coming to recreation;
let's all dance and sing and clap our hands in jubilation.
(Letters *no. 169:1, 449)*

TERESA INCORPORATED in her monastic constitutions a rule calling for an hour of daily recreation. She
felt it was extremely important for the nuns and friars
to have fun together. She knew that the community
would benefit, since a lightness of soul allows petty
grievances to be dissolved. It also facilitates a feeling of
solidarity and enables us to see one another in a new
light. No one's burden should be so great, she said, that
he or she can't free themselves from their exterior
duties or their interior workings for an hour.

A young nun sang the above quote as Teresa came
to recreation one day, for her presence was greatly valued. Teresa would spontaneously create songs and

encourage all the nuns to join her in singing them. Music was important to Teresa, and she bought many instruments for the monasteries so that the nuns could compose and play their own music. (Some of these instruments can still be viewed at the Incarnation Monastery in Avila.) She also favored dance, and it has been said that Teresa would take out her castanets, and creating her own accompaniment, dance the rhythms of her soul. What a beautiful image that brings to the mind: a nun in full habit letting the passion of her soul be expressed through her body.

Storytelling was another of Teresa's favorite recreational activities. She herself was known for her ability to captivate all present through her vivid descriptions and natural humor, but she also delighted in others' talents. She mentioned one young nun in particular, who, before coming to the monastery, had traveled to the Indies, and she would entertain them all with her stories about the people she met and her sea voyages. Teresa praised the nun for her storytelling abilities and wrote how all the nuns were grateful that she was a part of their community.

Recreation is literally a time to *re-create* our selves. A joyful freedom, when experienced by our whole being — soul, mind, and body — can effect change effortlessly. Old patterns that we have unconsciously encumbered ourselves with can break free, and we can encounter a new way of being. In the West recreation has come to mean time out to rest or to engage in our "get-fit" regimens. We would do well to look at our European counterparts who tend to enjoy their free time with dance, song, and storytelling. It is a time of communal creative joy and discovery, a time of delighting with, and in, one another. Souls are lightened, and natural creative natures are expressed.

We need to relearn how to do this. Just think how it would be if for an hour every day your community gathered and enjoyed each other, and I do not mean simply by talking, but by creating together. Unfortunately, many of us do not even know our neighbors, and giving more importance to our work, we feel we do not have time for fun. Perhaps this is why Teresa made recreation a rule in her constitutions; knowing human nature, she could see how other things could easily take precedence, with this vital ingredient of life being omitted. As we journey together, let us remember to have fun for fun's sake alone. There is no need to create a masterpiece or win a competition; we simply need to enjoy.

Meditation

Coming into your place of quiet, allow the lightness of your soul to come forward. Let it speak to you and show you how to express your natural creative self. Know that you can do whatever you are shown or whatever you feel the desire to do. Ask how you can take this newfound creativity into the community. Follow your fun!

65. God's Gentle Reminder

Eat for Me and sleep for Me,
and let everything you do be for Me,
as though you no longer lived but I. (CW vol. I, 414)

THIS JOURNEY WE HAVE EMBARKED ON never ends, not even for the angels or the saints. Every day is a new beginning, another opportunity for us to invite the spirit of God into our lives. The beauty lies in the simplicity of our task: letting this spirit guide us in everything we do. The above quote was a message from Christ to Teresa. By bringing the energy of Christ into our lives, we enter into the true power of love that transforms all it touches — most important, our own souls. This mystic reality, experienced through this gradual spiritual metamorphosis, now becomes a normal phenomenon. We can all share in this reality, regardless of our beliefs or racial backgrounds, since love is the ultimate place of perfect being.

Teresa did not always perceive God in a clear light, even late in her life. Sometimes fears and doubts would arise, and once she grew very anxious when she considered how little she had returned for having been given so much. Very quickly her anxiousness was allayed as she was reminded of the sacred marriage. All that belonged to God also belonged to her, she was told by Christ, and anything that she requested would be given. She became aware that God was now putting her soul in command, since being committed to doing God's will, it could not do anything else, even if it wanted. She understood that God could never be repaid for His generosity and that all that He required was to be loved.

Teresa had now entered the realm of true spiritual maturity; her own soul was divinely orchestrating her life. Yet simultaneously she was well aware that it was God who was achieving all. This is the blessed paradox of the human and divine incarnation. Without this knowledge — this ultimate act of humility — the soul remains in an illusion about its own effort. We must remember, said Teresa, that reaching this stage is well beyond our own power, and if we continue making an effort on our own, we will find our love growing cold.

Teresa, coming to the end of her journey here on earth, had become totally consumed by her love for God. She wrote that she no longer felt any attachment to people or the world, and she didn't suffer the intensity of her feelings as before, including her longings for God. She was no longer interested in seeking advice from others, or in giving it, and it mattered little to her whether she gained or lost anything and everything. She had reached the ultimate dwelling place of calm and peace. She was free from any desire other than to love. What has a soul to do but love more? she asked.

The knowledge that God and the soul are one is the basis of all mystical teachings. Living this knowledge, through loving every being as embodiments of the one spirit, is the perfection of these teachings. And it is through honoring and respecting each other that this love becomes manifest. May our hearts, like Teresa's, burn with love for God and for all His creation, knowing at once the greatness and the humbleness of who we are.

Meditation

Breathing deep into your being, call on the mystical grace of God. Let this grace permeate every part of your consciousness. Feel the majestic nature of who you are, and know that it is God who creates every part of your being. Allow a deep feeling of gratitude and love to rise within you. Take this love, along with honor and respect — for yourself and all beings — into the world.

Conclusion: The Ultimate Journey

As we journey through this life, into our death, and into life once more, we are constantly brought face to face with that ineffable place of surrender — the place where the past is allowed to dissolve and a new state of being is born. This is the place where our spirit can soar on the wings of God, if we bow our heads and hearts to the inner divine will. It is here that our chosen destiny and our place in the universe become assured. If we choose, however, to follow our own desires, we will fly with our own wings, and the journey will become long and arduous and very often meaningless. The choice is ours.

Teresa asks, "Do you know when people really

become spiritual?" and answers, "It is when they become slaves of God...[when] they have given Him their freedom" (*IC, 229*). It is too easy today, with spiritual and psychological theories abounding, for the modern man and woman to falsely believe that their lives are given to walking the spiritual pathway. Perhaps the true test of our spirituality is to ask, "Are we prepared to give God our freedom?" In the twenty-first century especially, freedom is one of our most precious commodities.

By following Teresa's words and advice, *and by putting both into practice,* we can build a solid foundation for our spiritual growth. Through perseverance, love, and humility, we will ultimately come to know, as Teresa did, that our true freedom does not consist of creating a personal paradise, but rather, of knowing that the Garden of Eden resides in God.

Resources

Bibliography

St. Teresa of Avila. *The Collected Letters of St. Teresa of Avila,* vol. 1. Translated by Kieran Kavanaugh, OCD. Washington, D.C.: ICS Publications, 2001.

——. *The Collected Works of St. Teresa of Avila.* Translated by Kieran Kavanaugh, OCD, and Otilio Rodriguez, OCD. 3 vols. Washington, D.C.: ICS Publications, 1976, 1980, 1985.

——. *Interior Castle: St. Teresa of Avila.* Translated and edited by E. Allison Peers. New York: Image Books, 1961.

————. *The Life of Saint Teresa of Avila by Herself.* Translated by J. M. Cohen. London: Penguin Books, 1957.

Jung, C. G. *Mysterium Coniunctionis.* Princeton: Princeton University Press, 1989.

Underhill, Evelyn. *Mysticism: The Nature and Development of Spiritual Consciousness.* Oxford: One World, 1993.

Recommended Reading

St. Teresa of Avila. *The Interior Castle.* Translated by Mirabai Starr. New York: Riverhead Books, 2004.

————. *Teresa of Avila: Selections from The Interior Castle.* San Francisco: HarperCollins, 2004.

Medwick, Cathleen. *Teresa of Avila: The Progress of a Soul.* New York: Knopf, 1999.

Acknowledgments

I WOULD LIKE TO THANK the following people for their support while I was writing this book. First, thanks go to Georgia Hughes at New World Library, for seeing beyond the first submission to the possibility of something greater; to Mimi Kusch, for contributing her fine and much-needed editorial skills; to all the staff at New World Library for their friendly and professional attention; and to John Nelson for educating me in the finer workings of the publishing world and for planting the seed for the format of this book.

Second, I would like to thank Brother Bryan Paquette at the Institute of Carmelite Studies for his patience and long-distance phone calls and Kieran

Kavanaugh, OCD, and Otilio Rodriguez, OCD, for their thorough and scholarly work on Teresa.

Third, thanks go to Kaila and James Nelson-Floto, Christina Fisher, and Joy Brisbane for their constant love and encouragement, and to Deborah Collins and Bert Esser for housing and feeding me and holding me in a warm and vibrant place of love while I wrote the book.

Fourth, I would like to thank my brother, Tony, and my sister-in-law, Jacqui, who held my hand in the dark times, and my nephews, Michael and Alec, for simply being there.

And finally, I wish to thank my dad, Bob Don, the most spiritual atheist I have ever known: thank you, for gifting me your strength of honesty and connection with the land. I still miss you twenty-four years after your passing. Thanks also go to my mum, Georgina Don, for giving her life to me, for instilling in me the wisdom of the Christian tradition without the rules and dogma, and for her never-ending support in every possible way. I extend my gratitude to you all, and to the very spirit of God, who patiently loves and guides me at every moment, even when I am looking the other way.

Permissions Acknowledgments

Excerpts from *The Collected Works of St. Teresa of Avila, Volume One* (copyright © 1976), *Volume Two* (copyright © 1980), and *Volume Three* (copyright © 1980), translated by Kieran Kavanaugh and Otilio Rodriguez, and *The Collected Letters of St. Teresa of Avila, Volume One* (copyright © 2001), translated by Kieran Kavanaugh, all copyright © by Washington Province of Discalced Carmelites, ICS Publications, 2131 Lincoln Road N.E., Washington, DC 20002-1199, www.icspublications.org. Reprinted by permission.

Excerpts from *Interior Castle* by Teresa of Avila, translated by E. A. Peers, reprinted by permission of Sheed &

Ward, an imprint of Rowman & Littlefield Publishers, Inc.

About the Author

MEGAN DON WAS BORN IN NEW ZEALAND, where she spent the first seventeen years of her life. She then left home and spent several years traveling to pursue her interests in spirituality and mysticism. When she was twenty-six she moved to Australia and converted to Catholicism. She became deeply involved with the Carmelite Order and began studying comparative religions and psychoanalytical studies at La Trobe University in Melbourne. In 2001, she visited Avila, Spain, to conduct research on St. Teresa for this book.

Megan is currently a spiritual counselor and teacher of "The Pathway of the Mystic."

If you enjoyed *Falling into the Arms of God*, we highly recommend the following titles from New World Library:

In the Heart of the World: Thoughts, Stories & Prayers by Mother Teresa

A collection of Mother Teresa's own written and spoken words on her life of service. Her pearls of spiritual truth are at times humorous, compassionate, and moving as she illuminates the sacredness found in the everyday tasks of living.

No Greater Love by Mother Teresa

A revealing and inspiring collection of Mother Teresa's personal thoughts on a broad range of spiritual topics including love, prayer, forgiveness, service, and Jesus.

The Mother Teresa Wisdom Deck: 50 Inspiration Cards

An inspiring deck of meditation cards that feature photographs of Mother Teresa and illuminating passages from her writings on joy, kindness, silence, generosity, faith, sacrifice, poverty, prayer, and love.

A Monk in the World: Cultivating a Spiritual Life by Wayne Teasdale

The author offers compelling insights into the practical and philosophical issues of his journey to a multifaith spirituality, providing inspiration for others on their own spiritual path.

The Mystic Heart: Discovering a Universal Spirituality in the World's Religions by Wayne Teasdale

An exploration of interspirituality that draws on the mystical core of the world's great religious traditions to form a new understanding of what it means to be spiritual. With a foreword by His Holiness the Dalai Lama.

The Mystic Hours: A Daybook of Interspiritual Wisdom & Devotion by Wayne Teasdale

A powerful daily guide to interspiritual wisdom with 365 quotes from the great religious and spiritual traditions, from sources as varied as St. John of the Cross, Confucius, and Allen Ginsberg, each followed by illuminating commentary by Teasdale.

For the Love of God: Handbook for the Spirit, Revised Edition edited by Benjamin Shield and Richard Carlson

A collection of writings by twenty-five of the world's most respected spiritual thinkers including Mother Teresa, the Dalai Lama, and Matthew Fox, describing what spirituality and God mean to them.

Promise Restored: Rediscovering the Ten Commandments in an Uncertain World by T. Wyatt Watkins

This book explores the relevance of the Ten Commandments in the ethics and moralities of our modern era. A must-read for any spiritual seeker interested in morality.

New World Library is dedicated to
publishing books and audio products
that inspire and challenge us to improve
the quality of our lives and our world.

Our products are available
in bookstores everywhere.
For our catalog, please contact:

New World Library
14 Pamaron Way
Novato, California 94949

Phone: (415) 884-2100 or (800) 972-6657
Catalog requests: Ext. 50
Orders: Ext. 52
Fax: (415) 884-2199

Email: escort@newworldlibrary.com
Website: www.newworldlibrary.com